# Metamorphosis:

# A Guide to the World Wide Web

# &

# Electronic Commerce

Version 2.0

**Patrick G. McKeown and Richard T. Watson**
**Department of Management**
**The University of Georgia**

John Wiley & Sons, Inc.
New York • Chichester • Brisbane • Toronto • Singapore

*To our children*

*Ashley and Chris*

*Alice, Ned, and Sophie*

| | |
|---|---|
| Acquisitions Editor | Beth Lang Golub |
| Marketing Manager | Leslie Hines |
| Senior Production Manager | Jeanine Furino |
| Senior Designer | Karin Kincheloe |
| Cover Designer | Carolyn Joseph |
| Manufacturing Assistant | Catherine Lao |
| Cover Photo | Comstock |

This book was set in 10/12 Palatino by Richard Watson and printed and bound by Banta Book Group. The cover was printed by Banta Book Group.

ISBN: 0-471-18032-7

Printed in the United States of America

10 9 8 7 6 5 4 3 2 1

# Preface

*Altavista.digital.com / Yahoo.com*

■■■■■■■■■■■■■■■■■■■■■■■■■■■■■■■■■■■■■■■■■■■

In describing *Metamorphosis: A Guide to the World Wide Web & Electronic Commerce*, the most important aspect we want to emphasize is that this is "not just another Web book!" Instead, it should be viewed from two perspectives. First, it provides a thorough overview of the Web and the Netscape Navigator browser including background on client/server networks, the Internet, browsers, accessing the Web, creating Web pages using HTML, and accessing Internet resources using the Web. Second, it demonstrates the impact that the Internet and the Web are having on businesses and organizations. It is this second aspect of the text that clearly sets it apart from many other guides to the Internet, the Web, and Netscape. In addition, there is a supporting Web site.[1] If you have not yet visited it, we suggest you do so in the near future. Five complete sites can be downloaded from the supporting Web site, and these can be used to support local Web access. Finally, there are many exercises throughout each chapter as well as end-of-chapter review questions and exercises.

Electronic commerce is clearly a rising tide in the world of business, and this book provides important information on how readers can take advantage of this trend to further their opportunities. The importance of being able to react positively to changes in technology is first discussed in Chapter 1 and then revisited in Chapters 6 and 7, where we discuss the fundamental principles of electronic commerce and provide practical answers to key questions about electronic commerce. Built around the concepts of the *customer service life cycle* and *integrated Internet marketing*, this approach provides the reader with a veritable *how to* manual on using the Web and Internet to further the aims of their organization. Without a doubt, Chapters 6 and 7 should be considered *required* reading for anyone interested in the coming world of electronic commerce.

In addition to the discussions on electronic commerce in Chapters 1, 6, and 7, almost 70 companies and organizations are used to demonstrate electronic commerce in action. In most cases, each organization's Web site URL is also provided. These same URLs are available by linking to the Web site for

---

1. http://www.negia.net/webbook

this book. By visiting these many commercial and organizational Web sites, the reader can gain great insight into the many ways the Web is being used.

Another unique aspect of this text is that the reader does not need to have access to the Internet and Web in order to learn about electronic commerce. This is made possible by the four commercial Web sites that can be downloaded from the supporting Web site to a local hard disk or file server from which they can then be accessed. These four sites include ScubaNet, Alberto's Nightclub, Rhebokskloof Estate Winery, and Jimmy Buffet's Margaritaville Store. In each case, the on-disk Web site includes many of the graphics found on the original Internet Web site. By accessing them in a local mode using the file:/// protocol, the reader can learn how the Web has been used commercially without taking up precious bandwidth. In fact, the book is set up so that the first four chapters can be covered without needing to access any remote Web sites. Only the later chapters require that the reader have access to remote Web sites. We believe that this feature will be especially important for those locales having limited or very slow Internet access or where many individuals might attempt to access the Web at the same time. This feature will enable the reader to experience and learn about the Web without depending on access to the Internet. In addition, a fifth local Web site demonstrates many advanced features of Netscape 3.x.

Another element of this text that will be of great use in the learning process is the *Your turn!* Exercises, which are placed strategically throughout each chapter to reinforce the learning process by asking the reader to implement some material just discussed in the text. In Chapters 2 and 3, the *Your turn!* exercises make heavy use of the five local Web sites mentioned earlier. In Chapter 4, the student is asked to practice writing HTML statements. Finally, in Chapters 5, 6, and 7 these exercises request that the student demonstrate an understanding of Internet resources and electronic commerce. In addition to the *Your turn!* exercises, there are review questions and exercises at the end of each chapter. Finally, there are key terms at the end of each chapter, which are defined in a Glossary at the end of the book.

## Acknowledgments

We would like to thank Tom Hall of Pitt Community College, Anthony Nowakowski of Buffalo State College, Jennifer Thomas of CUNY, Baruch College, Gigi Kelly of College of William and Mary, Cathy Beise of Kennesaw State University, and Karen Loch of Georgia State University for their outstanding reviews of the text. They made numerous useful suggestions. We would also like to thank Tonia Pearson and Katharina Vith of The University of Georgia for their close reading of the manuscript. At John Wiley & Company, we would like to thank our editor, Beth Golub. We would also like to thank Carolyn McKeown for her reading of parts of the original manuscript and Clare Watson for proofreading the entire text. We acknowledge the contribution of The University of Georgia electronic commerce research group: Sigmund Akselsen (visiting from Telenor, Norway), Issam L. Almutawaly, Traci Carte, Mutlu Celikok, Monica Garfield, Barbara Haley, and Erich Lehmair. Finally, we would like to thank our family and friends for their support during the writing and desktop publishing process.

Patrick G. McKeown
Richard T. Watson

# Table of Contents

# 1     Introduction to the Internet and World Wide Web

------------------------------------------------------------

**Objectives**

After reading this chapter, you will be able to:

❖ understand how computer networks will change the way we live and work;

❖ describe the emergence of electronic commerce and the resulting revolution in business;

❖ describe the Internet and its operations;

❖ describe the client/server relationship;

❖ discuss the World Wide Web and its impact on the Internet;

❖ understand the use of hypertext and multimedia on the Web;

❖ describe the use of Web pages and browser software;

❖ understand the importance of codification and distribution as they relate to information systems.

**Our networked world**

In less than four years, the 21st century will arrive on January 1, 2001. While we do not yet have the space ships and artificially intelligent computers portrayed in the movie *2001: A Space Odyssey*, we do have many other dramatic innovations not even considered in their wildest dreams by the creators of this movie. Specifically, computers and computer-controlled machines combined with high-speed communications media form **computer networks** that are dramatically changing the way we live and work. Whether you know it or not, you use computer networks on a daily basis. For example, when you go to an automatic teller machine (ATM) either in your home town or in another part of the world, a computer reads the magnetic strip on your card, compares it to the personal identification number (PIN) you key in, and decides if you are a valid user of that card. When you want to withdraw cash from the ATM, it has to make a connection with a local computer which in turn connects to your home bank's computer to verify that you can withdraw that amount of money. If you are in a foreign country, this involves a currency conversion between your home currency and that of the country in which you are withdrawing the money in the local currency. Through computer networks, this entire process can take less than a minute to carry out. Other computer networks with which you may deal on a frequent basis include long distance and cellular telephone systems, pager systems, airline, rental car, or hotel reservation systems.

It is becoming obvious that computer networks are going to alter our society every bit as much as introduction of the printed book altered medieval society 500 years ago. The printed book created a revolution of literacy that eventually resulted in people having the power to create today's democracies. It is altogether possible that the widespread availability of computer networks will result in a greater understanding of cultures that are different than our own. This in turn may lead to changes in our society even more radical than those brought about by the printed book. Already, in the few years since the computer network application known as the **World Wide Web** (or, simply, the **Web**) was introduced on a global scale in 1994, we are seeing the enormous changes that it has brought to our lives. For example, many television advertisements now include a subtitle that begins with the letters: **http://** indicating the address of the advertiser's Web site. They would like for you to use your computer to visit this Web site to find additional information about their product. Similarly, it is becoming quite common for your business card to have both an e-mail address and your personal Web page address in addition to your name, affiliation, telephone number, and postal address.

While long distance telephone networks have been with us for almost 100 years and television networks have been in existence for close to 50 years, neither of them has had as much effect on global information sharing as computer networks are already having. Actually, telephone and television networks are now essentially controlled by computers so they should also be included as computer networks. A world without computer networks would be dramatically different from that in which we currently live: no direct dial long distance telephone calls, no cable television programming—only local broadcast television, no access to our money through worldwide ATMs, no global access to electronic mail, and so on. You can surely think of other ways that computer networks have dramatically changed our lives over the last 20 years.

## Electronic communities

Today, the fastest growing computer network in the world is the **Internet**, which is a worldwide network of computers in which each computer agrees to use the same rules for sending and receiving information. The Internet has opened up the potential for individuals to use personal computers for entertainment, education, research, business, and communication with each other. Many names have been given to this network: data highway, infobahn, information superhighway, and so on. However, instead of a highway which we all know can be very boring, what is actually occurring is the creation of **electronic communities**, that is, exciting communities that are real in the sense that there are actual people but electronic in the sense that you can communicate with other members of the community without regard to who they are, where they live, or what time of day or night it is. Another name for this concept is **cyberspace** which was coined by William Gibson in his novel *Neuromancer*. The increasing use of the Internet is evidenced in numerous surveys. For example, in 1995, one such survey showed that computer users spent as much time using the Internet as they did watching rented video tapes.

One of the key elements of the Internet that creates the power of electronic communities is **many-to-many communication,** that is, a form of communication in which any person on the Internet can easily communicate with a large number of people also using it. This is a dramatic change from typical forms of communication which have typically been one-to-one (e.g., telephone calls) or one-to-many (e.g., newspapers, radio, and television). With many-to-many communication, everybody on the network can be a writer, a publisher, an artist, or an entertainer. While not everybody is a good writer or artist, there is still a tremendous amount of information that flows around the Internet each day. Much of this information is being displayed on the World Wide Web, which is the fastest growing use of the Internet.

## A different way of doing business

Within a few short years, many of us will find that our workplace will no longer be the traditional 8 to 5 office of the 20th century. In fact, you may find that you do not have a physical office or set work hours; instead, you may have a **virtual office** that exists wherever you happen to be at that time. In a virtual office, a person can be anywhere: at home, in a taxi, hotel room, or airline, or in an office space that is only used temporarily. In terms of technology changing the way we live, once you are no longer tied to an office, then you are able to live almost anywhere you wish as long as you have electricity and a telephone line.

Another aspect of the Internet that is changing the way we do business is the potential for **electronic commerce**, that is, *carrying out business transactions over computer networks*. While we have had some types of electronic business for several years including **electronic data interchange (EDI)** in which companies deal with each other electronically and the use of ATMs by consumers, these electronic business applications tend to be one-to-one or one-to-many rather than many-to-many as is possible over the Internet. Today, businesses of all types from around the world are looking for ways to use electronic commerce to generate revenue. For many companies, this involves finding ways to use the Web to advertise, sell, or support their products. The number of companies engaging in electronic commerce on the Web is growing at a rapid rate. One study[1] of the growth of electronic commerce has shown that between Fall 1994 and Fall 1996, the number of businesses with a presence on

---

1. Haley, B. J.; Carte, T. A.; Watson, R. T. Commerce of the Web: how is it growing? In: Proceedings of the Second AIS conference. 1996.

the World Wide Web grew from less than 500 to more than 33,000. There is a definite revolution going on in business as companies are trying to catch the wave of electronic commerce; those that fail may find themselves out of business.

## Creative destruction

Successful organizations in this time of rapid change will make the required transformation by creatively destroying old ways of interacting with customers, suppliers, employees, and shareholders, and then creating new ways. Like butterflies, who change from ugly caterpillars into beautiful creatures, organizations must effect a *metamorphosis* to a new type of business. Becoming a butterfly is a radical change for a caterpillar, and business must recognize that to exploit the opportunities created by information technology, it may have to undergo a similarly amazing metamorphosis—a radical redesign of current business practices.

Termed *creative destruction* by Harvard economist Peter Schumpeter, this concept emphasizes that the most important part of the change process for a business is not what *remains* after the change but what has been *destroyed*. Without a destruction of the old ways of carrying out business, we cannot create the new. Creative destruction often requires an entirely new way of thinking about the problems facing a business. Executives may need to redefine the problems or reframe the questions; simply doing business as usual will not suffice. For example, Reuben Mattus decided that he needed to creatively destroy his existing Bronx ice cream product in order to be successful. Rather than changing the ingredients or the formula, however, he changed the product name to Häagen-Dazs and raised the price. It did not matter that the name had no meaning in any language or that the same product now cost more, he had successfully redefined his approach to business.

## Computer networks

We stated earlier that computer networks have had a tremendous effect on global sharing of information. To understand why this has occurred, we first need to discuss computer networks in general. We will begin by classifying them as either centralized or decentralized. A **centralized computer network** is one in which there is one computer or a group of computers to which all other computers must be linked. Examples of centralized networks include the commercial computer networks like America Online and CompuServe. These commercial networks now serve millions of people who use personal computers to call into central computers to carry out a wide range of activities. For example, a user of one of these commercial networks can exchange information with other users on electronic bulletin boards or through *chat lines* read news reports, track the stock market, and make airline and hotel reservations. Figure 1-1 shows a typical centralized computer network.

A **decentralized computer network** is one in which there is no one computer or group of computers to which every other computer is linked. Instead, computers are linked to other computers which are linked to still other computers and so on. A decentralized network can also be composed of smaller networks, with each network having a central computer termed its **server**. Information is passed from one computer to another by passing

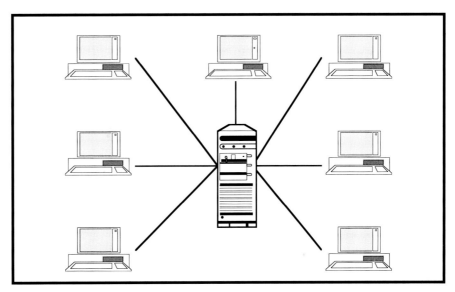

Figure 1-1. Centralized computer network

through intervening servers. Figure 1-2 shows a decentralized computer network.

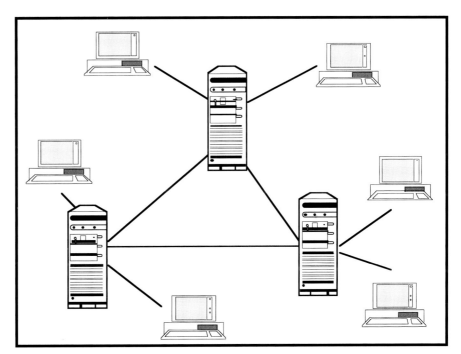

Figure 1-2. Decentralized computer network

A good way to compare centralized and decentralized computer networks is to consider the highly decentralized long distance phone system. In this system, when you place a call to a distant location, that call does not have to go to a central routing computer. Instead, it goes to the nearest telephone computer which decides the next leg in the routing. If one telephone computer goes down, the call can be instantly routed around it. On the other hand, the television networks are highly centralized in that national programming originates at a single location, say, New York, and if the power is out at that location, no one will receive the programming. For computers, both types of networks are necessary and useful. Centralized networks enable the dissemination of information and software from one central location; on the other hand, decentralized networks enable the many-to-many exchange of information and software which we said is driving the many changes we are now seeing in our world.

The Internet is the largest decentralized computer network, with millions of computers worldwide being linked together. The Internet is growing so rapidly that it is almost impossible to measure its exact size! Once restricted to professors and researchers for exchanging or searching for information, the Internet is now the most popular computer application at school, business, and home. In this chapter, we will introduce you to the Internet and its most popular element—the Web.

## The Internet: a network of networks

The Internet is actually a *network of networks* which links many small networks together. Each of these small networks agrees to use the same system of rules (called a **protocol**) for exchanging information. In addition, users on any network can exchange information with each other without having to know the physical location of the other user. The protocol for the Internet is called **TCP/IP**, which stands for Transmission Control Protocol/Internet Protocol. Each network that is linked to the Internet has at least one computer attached to it called a **host computer** that is capable of responding to requests for information or service from other computers on the Internet.

The amount and variety of information available on the Internet is tremendous, including millions of documents from individuals and organizations, e-mail lists, free software, access to other computers, discussion groups, drawings and photos, music and voice recordings, and video clips. While some of this type of information is also available on the centralized commercial networks, the sheer volume of available information is much greater on the Internet. For example, on the Internet, you can:

✤ send and receive messages to friends and relatives in a matter of minutes;

✤ find information on scuba diving locations around the world;

✤ listen to 3-minute previews of the newest Hootie and the Blowfish album;

✤ find and retrieve free software to create Web documents;

✤ work on a computer at a distant library to search its card catalog;

✤ buy shirts, hats, and other items from Jimmy Buffett's Margaritaville Store;

✤ obtain up-to-the-minute news, sports, and weather reports.

These are just a few examples of a virtually unlimited number of operations that can be carried out using the Internet. As you become more familiar with it, you will find many more that are particular to your needs and interests.

## Internet history

The Internet began in 1964 as the brainchild of a Rand Corporation researcher named Paul Baran who was seeking a method to ensure that the Pentagon could communicate with units of the U.S. armed forces in case of nuclear attack. It was assumed that links connecting any two cities would be completely unreliable, so he suggested a totally decentralized computer communications network with no central computer and no overall governing authority. In such a network, even if one or more computers were destroyed, it would still be possible to send information between remaining computers.

By the early 1970s, university faculty and other researchers found that, in addition to being a method of communicating with the U.S. armed forces, the Internet was an inexpensive way for them to communicate with each other. The Internet was made even more useful when the National Science Foundation (NSF) created a high-speed, long distance telecommunications network in the mid-1980s into which other networks could be linked. Although the NSF no longer supports this high-speed network, it is now supported by other organizations. The Internet made the news in 1988 when a Cornell graduate student unwittingly released a rogue program over it that caused some 6,000 Internet-connected computers to fail.

Until 1991, because the government subsidized the Internet, it was restricted to nonprofit, educational, and government organizations. In that year, NSF loosened those policies and allowed many new commercial sites, thus fostering the Internet's explosive growth. As a result, the commercial use of the Internet is an area of great interest to the many companies looking for business opportunities.

## Internet operations

As mentioned previously, the Internet is a great place for sharing information with other users, finding information from a variety of sources, acquiring software, or working on other computers. This can be done through five primary **Internet operations: file transfer protocol (FTP), e-mail, telnet, Internet newsgroups**, and the World Wide Web. While there are other Internet operations, these five are the most popular. These operations are shown in Table 1-1 along with an explanation of their use.

To carry out an Internet operation, you simply provide an address of a computer somewhere on the Internet to a software package on your computer. This software then contacts the distant computer and executes the requested operation. For example, if you wished to send a message to a friend at another university, you would use an e-mail software package. With this package, you would enter the address of their computer and a message. When you are finished, the software would send your message to their computer where they would use e-mail software to retrieve and read your message.

Table 1-1: Internet operations

| Internet operation | Purpose |
|---|---|
| FTP (File Transfer Protocol) | Retrieve files from a computer elsewhere on the Internet |
| e-mail (electronic mail) | Exchange electronic messages with other Internet users |
| Telnet | Work on a computer elsewhere on the Internet |
| Internet Newsgroups | Participate in a wide variety of on-line discussion groups |
| World Wide Web | Carry out all of the above operations as well as transferring text, images, sound, and video to a local computer |

## Accessing the Internet

To benefit from the wealth of information that is available on the Internet, you must first be able to access it with your personal computer. To do this, you must be linked to a regional network that is, in turn, linked to other networks on the Internet. All of these networks are linked into a primary high-speed communications line called the **backbone** that runs between major computer centers.

You can access the Internet either through your school or business or as an individual. If you access the Internet through your school or business, then your PC may be linked directly to a host computer which may be a mainframe or minicomputer. On the other hand, your computer may be linked into a **local area network (LAN)**. In either case, the mainframe/minicomputer or LAN is then linked to a regional network to which your school or business pays a fee to access the Internet.

Individuals who do not have organizational access to the Internet can access it either through a commercial network like America Online or CompuServe or through a new type of company called an **Internet service provider (ISP).** ISPs are companies that specialize in linking organizations and individuals to the Internet as well as providing other services to them. Today, many users of the commercial networks are only using them as service providers to access the Internet. In any case, the service provider provides the subscriber with software that enables them to access the Internet from their PC by calling the service provider using a device called a **modem**. Depending on the company, the user may pay an hourly fee for access time or a flat fee per month to access the Internet. Table 1-2 shows the fee structure for a typical ISP. Regardless of whether you are an organizational user of the Internet or an individual subscriber who is using a commercial network or Internet service provider, you do not need to be worried about the technical details of using the Internet. It is set up in such a way that if you know the address of the person or computer you wish to contact, the software on your local computer and on the computer you are accessing will take care of the rest.

Table 1-2: Typical Internet access costs

| Name of plan | Free hours | Additional hours | Monthly rate | Setup fee |
|---|---|---|---|---|
| Hourly | 20 | $1 per hour | $10.00 | $25.00 |
| Flat-rate | Unlimited | Unlimited | $19.00 | $25.00 |
| Corporate | Unlimited | Unlimited | $50.00 | $50.00 |

A good analogy to the Internet is the interstate highway system in the United States (which coincidentally, was also set up in the 1950s and 1960s to create a way of moving the U.S. armed forces around the country). To use the interstate system (which is equivalent to the national backbone of the Internet), you first have to traverse your local community highway system, then possibly your state highway system, and then finally get on an interstate highway. With both the Internet and the interstate highway system, you move from a local network to a regional network and then to a national or an international network. Figure 1-3 shows all of the ways a PC can be connected to the Internet: mainframe, LAN, and ISP.

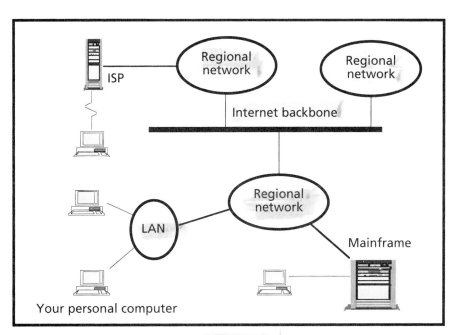

Figure 1-3. Typical connection to the Internet

## The World Wide Web

The newest addition to the Internet is the Web. Of all the changes to the Internet since its inception, the Web has brought the most radical changes and interest. Originally developed to allow scientists to easily exchange information, the Web is now the most popular application on the Internet as individuals and organizations find new and innovative ways to share information with others. The Web was developed in 1989 at the European Laboratory for Particle Physics (CERN) in Geneva, Switzerland, by a computer scientist who saw a need for physicists to be able to communicate with colleagues about their work while it was ongoing rather than waiting until a project was finished. To make this *real time* communications possible, he wanted to create an interconnected *web* of documents that would allow a reader to *jump* between documents virtually at will.

To do this, he turned to a concept known as **hypertext**, which is defined as a *method of linking related information in which there is no hierarchy or menu system.* In terms of documents, hypertext involves reading one document on the computer screen, finding a keyword of interest, clicking on that keyword with your mouse, and automatically being switched to another document that provides more information on that keyword. That new document can then be linked to other documents via hypertext, which are then linked to other documents and so on to create a web of documents. Figure 1-4 shows how hypertext works for documents.

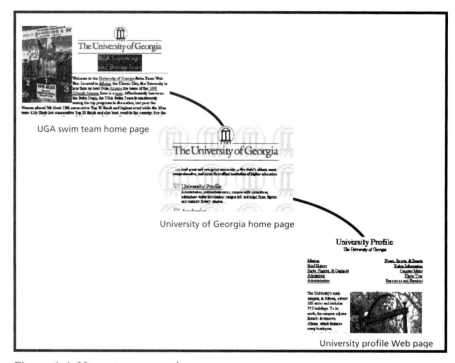

UGA swim team home page

University of Georgia home page

University profile Web page

Figure 1-4. Hypertext example

With hypertext, a user can navigate throughout the system limited only by his or her mental connections. For example, if you were reading a computer science text that implements a hypertext system and came upon a reference to Windows 95 that is indicated as a hypertext link, you could click on this keyword and be shown another page that discusses Windows 95 in more detail. You could then jump to a related discussion on using the mouse to make on-screen selections. From there, you might wish to jump to some other reference that interests you. Jumps within a document or to a completely different document are possible with hypertext, dependent only on the hypertext links created by the author of the documents. The World Wide Web is based on this concept of hypertext where documents are located on computers around the world and hypertext links are denoted in Web documents.

While very new to most computer users, hypertext actually predates the use of computers, with the original notion being proposed by President Franklin D. Roosevelt's science advisor, Vannevar Bush, in a 1945 *Atlantic* magazine article entitled "As We May Think." Twenty years later, computer visionary Ted Nelson coined the term *hypertext.* However, hypertext remained a largely hidden concept until Apple Computers released its Macintosh HyperCard software in 1987. If you have used the Microsoft Windows Help system, then you have already used hypertext to jump to other help screens by clicking on a highlighted keyword.

## Client/ server software

The Web is a special type of decentralized computer network: a **client/server network.** In a client/server (C/S) network there are two types of computers: clients and servers, with each running a different type of software. A **server** is a computer running a software application that manages a data store containing files of text, images, video clips, and sound. Servers are set up by organizations wanting to share information. A **client** is a personal computer running a software application that can access data on a server and display them. Flexibility is a great benefit of client/server, with clients and servers being able to run on a wide variety of computers and operating systems.

The power of the C/S networks is that the client and server form a dynamic duo to create a short-term partnership to satisfy needs for information. A client initiates the partnership by sending a request to a server for certain information. The server responds by retrieving the information from its disk and then transmitting it to the client. On receiving the data, the client formats the information for display. When preparing information for display, the client processes formatting instructions included in the file retrieved from the server. For example, assume that the creator of a document stored on a server has decided a certain phrase should appear in bold when displayed. The server cannot store the data in bold format, however. Instead, it has to store the data with some codes or tags to indicate which text will be in bold when displayed. For instance, the following character string stored on a server:

```
The <B>World Wide Web</B> is a new way of doing
business.
```

will be displayed by the client as:

  The **World Wide Web** is a new way of doing business.

because the client interprets the tag <B> as turn *on* bolding and the tag </B> as turn *off* bolding. The client/server process is shown in Figure 1-5.

Because clients and servers are set up to interact using a well-defined set of rules, any Web client can request data from any Web server. For instance, Web software running on a PC using Windows 95 can access files on a Macintosh or Unix-based server with no problems. A Web server can also store **multimedia files,** that is, digitized text, images, video, and sound. A client

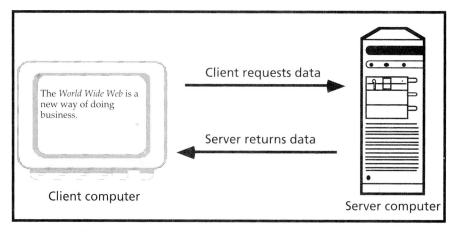

Figure 1-5. Client/server operation

retrieves these data, formats them, and converts them into appropriate human recognizable data. Thus, a client would convert a digitized sound file back to the sound of human speech or music (and, if we could digitize smells, a client could also reproduce those). The transfer of multimedia files from server to client is one of the key operations that sets the Web apart from the other Internet applications and is the major reason for the phenomenal growth of the Web. As of October 1996, one Web service was reporting that there were approximately 276,000 Web servers connected to the Internet and that the service was being accessed over 20 million times per weekday.[2]. Another study found that the number of Web servers was growing at the annual rate of 2,400%![3]

Each of the many servers on the Web has a unique address so that clients can specify where to find requested information. For instance, home.netscape.com is the address of the server computer for Netscape Communications Inc., the company that markets the most popular software for accessing the Web. Internet addresses will be discussed in more detail in Chapter 2.

## Using a browser with the Web

On the Web, the client software is called a **browser.** A browser can be used to fetch and read documents on-screen and print them, jump to other documents via hypertext, view images and listen to audio files. Web browsers use a **graphical user interface (GUI)** like that available on Microsoft Windows or the Apple Macintosh. With a GUI-based Web browser, you can perform various operations simply by pointing at menu selections or icons representing operations and clicking the mouse button—so-called **point and click operations**. For example, you can use a browser to navigate the Web by pointing at

---

2. http://altavista.digital.com/

3. MCI Communications Corp, Washington, DC and Network Wizards, Menlo Park, CA as quoted in "ISP Internet Service Problems?," *Computerworld*, July 8, 1996, p. 53.

a hypertext link in the current document and clicking on it. This operation causes the linked document, image file, or audio file to be fetched from a distant computer and displayed or played on the local computer. While not a point and click operation, you can also enter an address to retrieve a desired document or file.

There are a large number of browsers currently available for working on the Web using a PC, Macintosh, or Unix-based computer. However, the two most popular Web browsers are the Netscape Navigator and the Microsoft Internet Explorer, with Navigator controlling the largest share of the browser market. Both Navigator and Explorer can be obtained free of charge for academic use. Early or *beta* versions of these browsers can also be downloaded. In both cases, no technical support is available to the user. The final versions of the browsers can also be purchased for less than $50, in which case technical support is available. Figure 1-6 shows the Netscape Navigator browser. Other applications will be discussed as we proceed through the book.

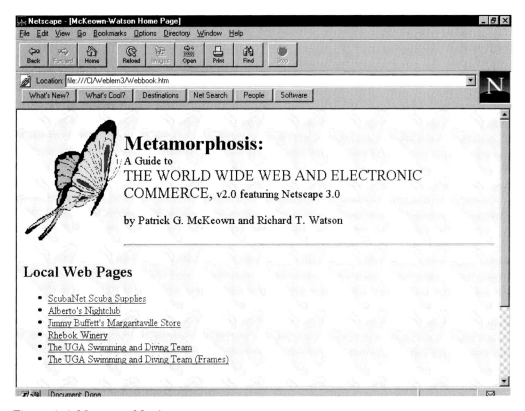

Figure 1-6. Netscape Navigator

While the primary purpose of a browser is to navigate the Web, it also can be used for the four other Internet operations—e-mail, FTP, telnet, and newsgroups. For example, with a Web browser, a user can use FTP to access and retrieve *(download)* an extensive amount of free software that is available on the Internet. This software has been placed on server computers specifically for downloading by Internet users. Because a browser can be used to carry out all of these operations, it is the *Swiss Army knife* of the Internet. By this we mean that while specialized client software, say an e-mail package, may do a better job on a specific operation, you could get by very well with just a Web browser.

*Web pages*      The primary purpose of a Web browser is to retrieve electronic documents from Web servers and to display them on a client computer. These electronic documents, called **Web pages**, are stored on server computers called **Web sites**. Web pages contain specially marked text and hypertext links to **multimedia** elements and to other Web pages. In addition to being electronic rather than physical, Web pages are different from pages in a book or magazine in other ways. For example, while the amount of information on a physical page is restricted to the size of the paper page, a Web page can extend beyond that shown on the screen. Table 1-3 shows the differences between electronic Web pages and physical pages.

Table 1-3: Differences between a Web page and physical page

| Characteristic | Web page | Physical page |
|---|---|---|
| Form | Electronic | Ink on a paper page |
| Amount of information | Can extend beyond a single screen | Restricted to one piece of paper |
| Types of information | Can include text, images, audio, and video information | Restricted to text and images |
| Links to other pages | Can be linked to an unlimited number of Web pages through hypertext | Can be linked only through a separate index |
| Creation | Can be created through a markup language and saved to a computer | Can be created using a word processor, desktop publishing, and laser printer |

Web users can access and display pages using their browser. In many ways, Web pages are at the heart of the Web since they provide users with the information that is unique to the Web. The browser in Figure 1-6 is shown displaying the Web page for this textbook. In addition to displaying text documents, a browser can be used to display graphics and photos and to play music and video clips directly without first having to switch to different software packages for each element. When you select a hypertext link to one of these elements, the browser executes a helper software program that works with that type of multimedia. Figure 1-7 shows a Web page with photographic images being displayed by a Web browser.

Many individuals, companies, and organizations have created Web pages that contain information about themselves and their activities, and more

Figure 1-7. Photographic image displayed by Web browser

pages are added to the Web every day. In October 1996, the same service mentioned earlier reported there were 30 million Web pages.[4] There are now numerous services whose sole purpose is to track pages that are on the Web and to make their addresses available to Web users. As discussed earlier, the number of commercial Web sites is also growing at a dramatic rate. Four interesting business applications on the Web are discussed in a later section and will be used for demonstration purposes throughout this book.

## The revolution in business

At the beginning of this chapter, we introduced you to the concept that before businesses can effect meaningful change, they must destroy their current practices or the competitive world will do it for them. No longer is evolutionary change acceptable. Companies must make revolutionary changes to take full advantage of the information technology now available. There are two basic principles of data that you must understand in order to comprehend the forces impelling this revolution: codification and distribution.

**Codification** describes an organized method for storing data in a computer system. Initially, only alphabetic characters, numbers, and special char-

---

4. http://altavista.digital.com/

acters were coded. For example, in ASCII, a popular coding system, each character is represented by a unique 8-bit code. More recently, codification has been extended to include multimedia objects such as images, video, and audio. Thus, on a computer you can store photos of people, videos of a space shuttle blast-off, and a sound clip from a CD.

**Distribution** describes how widely information is shared. Several technologies have enabled widespread sharing of information: fiber optics, compression, and networks. Fiber optic cable, with its high communication capacity and low cost, means vast quantities of information can be transported inexpensively. Compression methods, which permit the size of large files to be substantially reduced, make it feasible to transport multimedia objects electronically. Finally, the development of local and world wide networks has created the infrastructure for linking all computers in the world. The combination of these three technologies has made possible the widespread distribution of information.

Figure 1-8 shows that many classes of information systems can be conveniently described by the interaction of codification and distribution where codification goes from low (character only) to high (multimedia) and distribution ranges from local to global. A management information system (MIS) is typically a firm-wide system that provides character-based reports to managers. An MIS falls in the bottom left corner because of its low level of codification (character only) and low distribution (internal to a firm). An executive information system (EIS) is an extension of the MIS idea to meet the special needs of senior executives. Since many EISs include multimedia features (such as charts), they have a high level of codification, but they remain local to an organization.

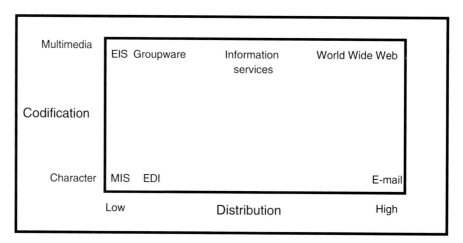

Figure 1-8. Codification and distribution

Electronic data interchange (EDI), character-based electronic communication between trading partners, provides wider information distribution than an MIS because it extends beyond the boundary of one company. It is e-mail, however, that supports the widest distribution of character-based information. The Internet permits widespread global text communication between any two or more people with Internet access—which currently includes millions of people.

Groupware, and Lotus Notes in particular, is a step forward in the wider distribution of multimedia. Some Notes applications span several organizations. Information services, such as America Online and CompuServe, provide an even wider distribution of multimedia information. For example, America Online offers hundreds of interactive information services to its millions of subscribers.

The Web, with its hundreds of thousands of servers accessible by more than tens of million people, is larger than any commercial information service. Furthermore, nearly all commercial services have embraced the Web by offering connections to it. There are other facets of the Web that make it substantially different from commercial services. The Web is a decentralized network—it is very easy for new Web services to be connected, and they do not need the approval of a central authority. The Web is global—a Brazilian consumer can order fish from an Icelandic salmon merchant or a sports fan in Hong Kong can check the latest soccer scores in Europe with equal ease. The Web has spawned a high degree of entrepreneurial, innovative activity. The combined intelligence of millions of people is creating a highly fertile forum for news.

Because the Web supports a new class of information systems—wide distribution of multimedia— and because it is a breeding ground for innovation, we believe that it represents a business revolution. Businesses are discovering that the Web is a new technology for marketing and delivering products and services. As companies exploit this new technology, the competitive forces of free markets and private enterprise will power tremendous change in business. Already, for instance, some catalog companies have discovered that Web ordering is one-third the cost of traditional phone ordering. Businesses have found that they can distribute information to customers in minutes instead of days. There is a large-scale project in Silicon Valley to facilitate electronic commerce between high-technology firms. These few examples, and many more discussed in this book, foretell tremendous change.

Look back at Figure 1-8 and contemplate the change that occurred when an organization introduced an MIS, EDI, or e-mail. Now, speculate about what will happen when we move to the right-top corner of the information codification-distribution grid. We trust you are convinced that we are about to commence a business revolution. Now is the time for you to develop the skills to be an active player in this revolution.

## Commerce on the Web

As noted above, commerce on the Web is becoming big business. In this book, we will use four commercial Web sites to demonstrate this trend. These four sites are:

❖ ScubaNet

❖ Rhebokskloof Winery

❖ Alberto's Nightclub

❖ Jimmy Buffett's Margaritaville

Let's take a brief look at the four companies whose Web sites we will use to demonstrate commerce on the Web.

Located in Fort Lauderdale, Florida, ScubaNet is an on-line provider of scuba equipment and boats. An example of scuba-oriented swimsuits available from ScubaNet was shown earlier in Figure 1-7.

Rhebokskloof Estate is found at the northern end of the Paarl Valley in one of South Africa's best wine-producing areas. Virtual visitors can tour the winery, visit the wineshop, and check out the three restaurants on the estate. We recommend the Cape Dutch Homestead if you would like to sample the local fare. You can also read about the several red and white wines offered for sale and even place an order.

Experience the atmosphere and excitement of Alberto's Nightclub. The Mountain View, California, nightclub provides live music and shows. Learn about the rhythms of the Salsa, and check out the dance instructors—Alex and Nicole.

For many fans around the world, Jimmy Buffett's music epitomizes a lifestyle which they would like to attain. Now, parrotheads, as Buffett's fans like to be called, have their own Web page. Sponsored by Jimmy Buffett's Margaritaville, a store in Key West, Florida, this page has many features, including an information source called the Coconut Telegraph, a list of records under Jimmy's own Margaritaville label, a list of tour dates, a section devoted to the environment, and a section for ordering a wide variety of Jimmy Buffett wearing apparel using an electronic order form.

In addition to these four commercial Web sites, we will use the Web site for the University of Georgia swim team to demonstrate a variety of features of browsers and the Web. Created by Jeff Wood, a student at the University, this Web site uses many of the advanced features of the Web in its presentation of information about the nationally ranked UGA swim teams.

## A road-map to this book

The six upcoming chapters should be read sequentially. Chapter 2 discusses the use of browsers to access the Web while Chapter 3 covers the use of a specific browser, Netscape, in detail. Chapter 4 covers the design and construction of home pages, and Chapter 5 discusses advanced browser operations, including searching for information on the Internet. Finally, Chapters 6 and 7 return to the topic of commerce on the Web, discussing electronic commerce fundamentals and managing electronic commerce.

A unique feature of this systematic ordering is that the reader is able to go through the first four chapters without requiring access to remote sites on the Web. To do this, the Netscape Navigator browser is used to access local Web pages stored on a hard disk. Also, a text editor is used to create home pages that are stored on a floppy disk. If the reader has access to the Web, then in Chapter 5, Netscape can be used to access various Web pages, carry out search operations, and access Internet operations.

## Key terms and concepts

backbone
browser
centralized computer network
client
client/server network
codification
computer network
cyberspace
decentralized computer network
distribution
electronic commerce
electronic communities
electronic data interchange (EDI)
e-mail
FTP (File Transfer Protocol)
graphical user interface (GUI)
host computer
hypertext
Internet

Internet Newsgroups
Internet operations
Internet service provider (ISP)
local area network (LAN)
many-to-many
   communication
modem
multimedia files
page
point and click operations
protocol
server
TCP/IP
telnet
Virtual office
Web
Web page
Web site
World Wide Web

## Exercises

1. How are computer networks changing the way we live and work? Name at least one other than those mentioned in the text.

2. What is the principle of creative destruction? What does it have to do with business and industry?

3. Why is the Internet referred to as a "network of networks"? What is a protocol and what does it have to do with the Internet?

4. What is TCP/IP? Why do we relate the Internet to the U.S. interstate highway system?

5. Discuss common ways that users have access to the Internet. Which method do you have?

6. List the important applications of the Internet. Which have you already used?

7. What does hypertext have to do with the World Wide Web? What type of software is necessary to be able to use the Web?

8. What type of interface does Web software offer the user?

9. What is hypertext? How is it implemented on the World Wide Web?

10. What type of information is available on the Web? What is a Web page? What is a Web site?

11. What are some of the differences between a Web page and a physical page?

12. What is a client/server network? What purpose does the server accomplish in a C/S network? What does C/S have to do with the Web?

13. What is a browser? What is its primary purpose?

14. How do browsers handle multimedia? Why do we refer to browsers as the *Swiss Army knives* of the Web?

15. What are codification and distribution? What do they have to do with types of information systems?

16. What are codification and distribution? What do they have to do with types of information systems?

# 2    Introduction to browsers

- - - - - - - - - - - - - - - - - - - - - - - - - - - - - - - - - - - - -

**Objectives**

After reading this chapter, you will be able to:

- ❖ discuss the use of browsers to access the Web;
- ❖ describe the elements of a browser;
- ❖ understand Internet addresses and URLs;
- ❖ discuss the types of files that are part of a Web page;
- ❖ describe key operations that can be performed with a browser;
- ❖ access Netscape in a Windows system;
- ❖ use Netscape to access a Web page.

**Introduction**

As discussed in Chapter 1, the Web is the newest and fastest growing part of the Internet with the number of Web servers providing information growing at a rapid rate. In March 1995, the volume of traffic over the Web surpassed that of e-mail, the previous volume leader. Dr. Larry Smarr, Director of the National Center for Supercomputer Applications (NCSA), has predicted that by the year 2000, close to *1 billion* people will have personal computers (up from less than 200 million in 1995) and that virtually all of these people will be on the Web.[1] He went further and stated that all of these people will be reading documents available on the Web and publishing information themselves. While Dr. Smarr's prediction *may* be overly optimistic, undoubtedly we are moving into a true *information age*

---

1. Larry L. Smarr, "The creation of cyberspace: how the Internet will change your life," The University of Georgia, May 3, 1995.

21

and the Web is the catalyst that is making this move possible. For business, the Web is opening up new horizon for commerce that had not been previously considered. For those companies willing to make the metamorphosis, the Web will bring very positive results.

Recall from Chapter 1 that the Web is a **client/server network** on which server computers make documents available to users running client software on their personal computers. The client software that is used to access, display, save, and print the documents stored on servers located anywhere in the world is called a **browser**. It is so named because this software allows the user to *browse* the many Web servers around the world. Recall also that these are not just ordinary sequential text documents; rather, the documents available on Web servers make wide use of both hypertext and **multimedia.** Figure 2-1 shows how a browser displays a document with information about Jimmy Buffett's Margaritaville.

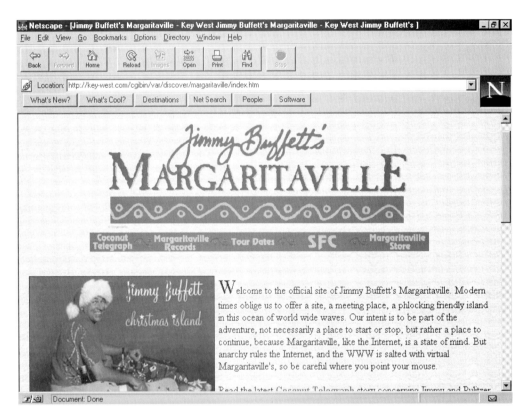

Figure 2-1. Jimmy Buffett's Margaritaville

**Hypertext** is a nonsequential method of linking related information; this means you can jump from document to document by following a trail of hyperlinks that represent areas of interest to you. Another element of Web documents that distinguish them is the wide use of multimedia, that is, *an interactive combination of text, graphics, animation, images, audio, and video dis-*

*played by and under the control of a personal computer.* On the Web, multimedia makes Web documents much more interesting and informative than a book or magazine. When you view a Web document, you can see a picture or graphic element, hear an audio clip or even view a video clip that provides additional information to the text in the document. In many Web documents, hypertext and multimedia are combined to create **hypermedia**. With hypermedia, a user can click on a graphic image and hear an audio clip or click on a word in the document and see an animation. In the case of the Web document shown in Figure 2-1, the hypertext links are represented by underlined words or phrases, and the graphical and photographic images represent a form of multimedia.

## The evolution of Web browsers

A key element that has enabled the Web to become such a popular vehicle for sharing information is the graphical browser client software like Netscape Navigator and Microsoft Explorer. Graphical browsers make it easily possible for users to find and display hypermedia Web documents. While there are nongraphical browsers like Lynx, when we refer to *browsers* in the future, we are referring to graphical browsers. Without them, it is extremely doubtful that the Web would have become as popular as it is now.

To understand the impact of Web browsers, consider the effect they have had on the growth of traffic on the Internet. After 15 years of relative obscurity as a network used primarily by defense researchers, the Internet started to grow in 1986 when the National Science Foundation funded the first high-speed communications *backbone* linkage between five supercomputer centers across the country. This allowed many universities to be linked into the Internet resulting in a significant growth in traffic over the network. This growth was increased in 1992 when commercial organizations were also allowed to link into and use the Internet. The real growth in the Internet has occurred since 1993 when the first widely available graphical browser, Mosaic, allowed people to explore the World Wide Web. At NCSA, the Internet traffic increased by a factor of *100,000* between the introduction of Mosaic and Spring of 1995.[2] Figure 2-2 shows the growth of the Internet in terms of number of host computers connected to it.

### Problems with the Internet

To understand why browsers have had such a dramatic impact, you need to know that prior to the introduction of the Web and browsers, many people found the Internet difficult to use. There were several reasons for this, including the fact that the Internet was (and still is) based primarily on computers running an operating system called Unix, and it required separate software packages for each application.

In the first case, while Unix is a very powerful operating system for working with networks of computers, it is anything but *user friendly*! In fact, unless a graphical user interface such as X-Windows is used, using Unix requires a knowledge of text commands which must be typed into the computer in the

---

2. Ibid.

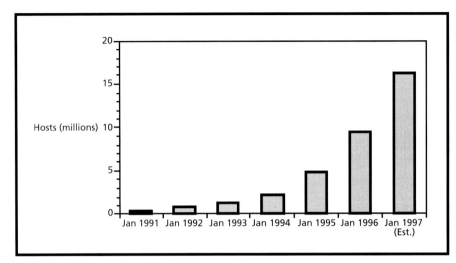

Figure 2-2.  Growth of the Internet since 1991

same way that DOS commands were needed on PCs before the introduction of Windows. While Unix commands were not a problem for many early users of the Internet who were professors or scientists, they did discourage widespread use. For example, to download a file from another computer, you had to use appropriate commands to navigate the various directories to find the file, enter a command to define the file as being text or binary (machine language) file, and then use the appropriate command (GET) to download the file to your computer. While there are some Windows-based and Macintosh applications that allow the use of a point and click interface, other Unix-based Internet software applications still require a command line interface.

A second problem with using the Internet was that users had to have a separate software program or client for each of the applications on the Internet. Recall from Chapter 1 that these applications included **FTP, e-mail, Telnet,** and **newsgroups** (or simply **News**). Before the creation of Web browsers, no single software program could handle all these applications. This meant that separate software applications had to be installed on each computer and users had to learn a variety of commands to use the individual applications.

Finally, because Unix-based Internet was primarily text-based, it was directed at displaying text and numbers, not graphics or photos or playing music or videos. While it was (and still is) possible to download files containing photos or music from Internet computers, it was not possible to play them on the same software that was used for the downloading. It was necessary to shift to another piece of software to view the photo or to play the music file.

Web browsers solved all of these Internet problems. Table 2-1 shows the problems with the Internet plus the solutions provided by Web browsers. A browser with its graphical interface is easy to use, with no need to learn arcane Unix commands. Browsers are also capable of carrying out virtually all applications mentioned previously, thereby eliminating the need for multiple software packages. Finally, browsers can both download and display images as well as play audio and video files. By solving these problems with the

Internet, Web browsers have made it easy and fun for many more people to have access to the virtually unlimited amount of information that is available on the Internet. The capability of Web browsers to carry out all of these operations is the reason why we called it the Swiss Army Knife of the Internet.

Table 2-1: Web browser solutions to Internet problems

| Problem | Web browser solution |
|---|---|
| Unix operating system | Easy-to-use GUI software |
| Requires separate software packages | Browser does it all |
| Orientation toward text and numbers | Browser handles multimedia as well as text |

## History of browsers

As mentioned in Chapter 1, the Web was developed at CERN in Switzerland in 1989. The first browsers were text-based packages that ran only on Unix machines. A hypertext link was selected by entering a number that retrieved a corresponding document. While text-based browsers such as Lynx are still used for many text-only applications, they have been rapidly eclipsed by graphical browsers for multimedia applications.

Realizing a trend in personal computers toward graphical interfaces on Windows for PCs and Macintosh computers, a group of students at the University of Illinois working at NCSA began to create a graphical browser. Led by Marc Andreeson, this group developed a graphical browser called *Mosaic*. First released in February 1993, for Unix-based workstations, Mosaic was also available for Macintosh and Windows-based machines by the Fall of 1993. Because Mosaic was developed by a publicly funded research facility, it was made available to Internet users free of charge. The meteoric growth of the Web discussed earlier and shown in Figure 2-2 was a direct result of the wide availability of free browser software. This policy of freely giving away browsers has continued to be followed for noncommercial users of Netscape Navigator and Microsoft Explorer.

While not the first graphical browser, the development of Mosaic is considered by many to be the key event that led to the widespread use of the Web. A December 1993, article in the *New York Times* referred to Mosaic as the *killer application of the Internet*; however, like other *killer apps* such as the VisiCalc spreadsheet and the dBASE database management software that initially controlled their market, Mosaic generated competition that has far surpassed it in numbers of users. In the case of Mosaic, Marc Andreeson and some of his fellow students left NCSA and joined computer industry executives to form a company dedicated to creating a better browser. Netscape Navigator, the result of this work, was released in Fall 1994. As with Mosaic, Navigator is available free of charge to noncommercial users. The company, Netscape Communications, Inc., generates revenue by selling Navigator to commercial users. It also sells the server software necessary to distribute Web documents as well as other software needed to publish Web documents.

Netscape Navigator offered many improvements over the original Mosaic and has become the most popular browser in use today with the company claiming over 38 million users[3]. However, Netscape is now facing stiff competition from Microsoft, the largest software company in the world. In 1996, Microsoft CEO Bill Gates dedicated Microsoft to becoming as big a force in Internet software as it is in operating systems and application software. As a result of this effort, in a relatively short time, Microsoft Internet Explorer has grown to be second only to Netscape Navigator in number of users. Netscape is not resting on its laurels and is working to improve Navigator in order to continue its dominance in the market. Because of its widespread use, we will use Netscape Navigator in this text to demonstrate the use of browsers. Figure 2-3 compares Navigator and Explorer for the ScubaNet Web page.

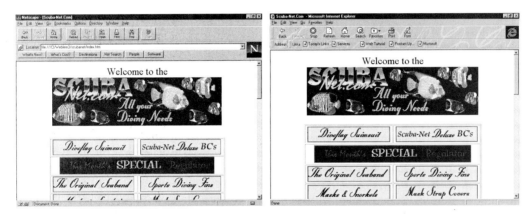

Figure 2-3. Netscape Navigator and Microsoft Internet Explorer

## Using browsers

Information is available on the Web primarily as documents called Web pages. As mentioned in Chapter 1, a **Web page** is a special type of document that contains hypertext links to other documents or to various multimedia elements. Some multimedia elements like graphics and images are actually displayed in the Web page. Others are played separately from the Web page. Web pages are retrieved from Internet server computers commonly referred to as **Web sites**. The first page you encounter when you visit a Web site is the **home page,** from which you can explore other Web pages that have been linked to it. For example, the Web page shown earlier in Figure 2-1 is the home page for Jimmy Buffett's Margaritaville Web site, and the Web page shown in Figure 2-3 is the home page for the ScubaNet Web site.

Web pages are created using a set of special tags called the **Hypertext Markup Language (HTML)**. HTML is used to create the format of the Web pages in terms of boldfacing, underlining, and sizes of headings. HTML is also used to create the links between Web pages and between Web pages and multimedia elements. HTML is discussed in detail in Chapter 4.

---

3. Navigator tops 38m users worldwide, *The Bangkok Post Database*, June 26 1996, p. 4.

## Browser elements

In looking at Figure 2-3, you can see that both Navigator and Explorer have many elements in common. To discuss these elements, consider Figure 2-4 which points out many of them in Netscape Navigator for the UGA swim team home page. These are also shown in Table 2-2, with a short description of each. Other elements are discussed in Chapter 3.

Table 2-2: Summary of browser screen elements

| Netscape element | Description |
| --- | --- |
| Title bar | Contains the title of the Web page |
| Menu bar | Contains main menu options |
| Toolbar | Buttons activate important Netscape commands |
| Location window | Displays the address of the current Web page |
| URL link icon (Windows 95 only) | Dragable icon that represents the address in the location window |
| Status indicator | Displays animated logo when page is being retrieved |
| Directory buttons | Buttons provide access to interesting or useful Web pages |
| Content area | Displays the contents of the Web page |
| Hypertext link | Links the Web page to another Web site |
| Scroll bars | Scrolls the Web page up and down |

We will briefly discuss the function of each of these browser elements. You do not need to learn how to use all of them since, in many cases, they provide different ways of doing the same thing. In fact, Netscape gives you the option to remove some of them from the screen if you find them unnecessary. (However, do not modify the Netscape screen in a computer lab environment without first checking with your instructor.)

In looking at Figure 2-4, the **title bar** at the top of the screen displays the title of the Web page you have retrieved. In this case, the title bar shows that the home page is titled "Netscape -[Welcome - The UGA Swimming and Diving Team]". If no page has been loaded, the title page will simply display *Netscape*. Beneath the title bar is the **menu bar** which is used to execute commands. Nine of these commands can also be executed using the **toolbar buttons** located immediately below the menu bar. Below the toolbar is the **location window** which contains the **Web page address** that is used to retrieve this Web page. In Windows 95 only, there is a dragable icon to the left of the location window that represents the Web page address. Below the Web page address are the **directory buttons** that provide links to interesting and helpful pages. The Web page itself is displayed in the **content area.** The **mouse pointer** in the shape of an arrow is used to move around the Web pages. **Scroll bars** on the right side and bottom of the main screen allow you to move to parts of the Web page that are not currently on the screen. While

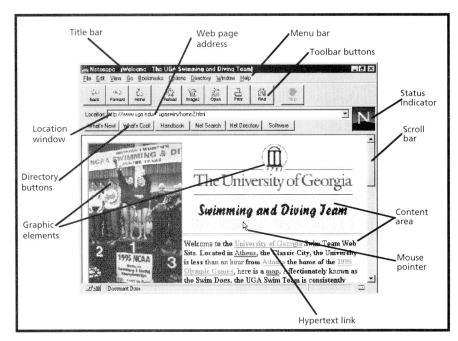

Figure 2-4. Browser elements

we refer to documents on the Web as *pages*, they are usually much longer than a single page of information. For that reason, you need to use the vertical scroll bar to move up and down the Web page. You will also note the numerous **graphic elements** in Figure 2-4, including the logo for the University of Georgia and a photo of the 1995 NCAA Championship 200 Freestyle Relay team from Georgia. While not shown in this figure, home pages can also have audio or video elements that can be played by clicking on an icon.

Note that some words or phrases are underlined in the Web page. These underlined elements are the clickable **hypertext links.** When you move the pointer to a clickable link, the pointer changes to a pointing finger and the address of that link is shown at the bottom of the browser screen. Clicking on a hypertext link enables you to jump from the current Web page to other pages, multimedia elements, or other Web resources. (The clickable links are also in color, which you cannot see on this black-and-white page.) They also can be links to other parts of the current document. These latter links act like a *hyper table of contents* that allow you to go to any other part of the document by simply clicking on the link.

Two colors distinguish hypertext links, often blue and purple. Blue links correspond to Web pages or parts of the same page that have not yet been visited, while purple links correspond to Web pages that have been visited recently. These distinguishing colors are very useful when you jump from page to page and cannot remember which links have been followed. Icons or images also can be used as hypertext links, which are often indicated by a colored border. In Figure 2-3, the ScubaNet Web page uses boxes with product names or categories as hypertext links. Clicking on such an icon or image will have the same effect as clicking on an hypertext link. Quite often there are links to pages created other developers; providing links to related pages is a common method of providing more information on a topic. For example, in Figure 2-4, there are links to Atlanta and the University of Georgia sites.

When the mouse pointer is positioned over a hypertext link, it changes to a pointing finger indicating that this is a link. At the same time, the address of the linked Web page appears at the bottom of the browser screen. Figure 2-5 shows the mouse pointer positioned over the University of Georgia's hypertext link in the swim team home page. Note that the address of the corresponding Web page (http://www.uga.edu/home.html) is displayed at the bottom of the screen. Figure 2-6 shows the Web page that results from clicking on this hypertext link. Note that the Web page address in the location window for this page matches the address shown at the bottom of the previous page.

Figure 2-5. Mouse pointer positioned over hypertext link

## Browser operations

With a browser, you can perform several key operations to access the information that is available on the Internet. These operations include:

❖ retrieving a home page;

❖ connecting to other Web pages via hypertext links;

❖ navigating among Web pages;

❖ retrieving previously viewed Web pages;

❖ searching for interesting Web pages;

❖ saving and printing Web pages;

❖ using e-mail, forms, and maps.

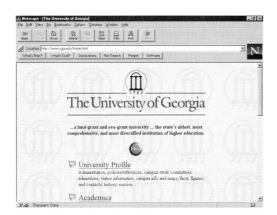

Figure 2-6. Result of clicking on a hypertext link

We will discuss the first operation—retrieving a home page—in some detail. We will then briefly discuss each of the other operations. Finally, we will discuss how to access Netscape and use it to retrieve a home page and then connect to another Web page. In Chapter 3, we will show how to use Netscape to carry out each of these operations. In Chapter 5, we will discuss a variety of advanced browser operations.

Because graphical browsers run under Microsoft Windows on IBM-compatible PCs, on Apple Macintosh computers, or on X-Windows Unix workstations, a graphical user interface (GUI) is used to work with them. A mouse or trackball can be used to select options from menus or to click on buttons to perform browser operations.

## Retrieving a home page

A Web home page is accessed by an address. In Web terminology, the address of a home page is referred to as its **URL** (for **Uniform Resource Locator**). It is so named because a URL is a standard means of consistently locating Web pages or other resources no matter where they are stored on the Internet. For example, the URL of the UGA swim team home page shown in Figure 2-1 is:

http://www.uga.edu/~swimteam/home2.html

and the URL of the ScubaNet Web site shown in Figure 2-3 is:

http://wahoo.webrunner.net/index.html

Like every URL, this one has four parts: the protocol, the Internet address of the server computer on which the desired resource is located, the port number (optional), and the path of the resource. Three parts of the UGA swim team address (which does not have a port number) are shown in Figure 2-7.

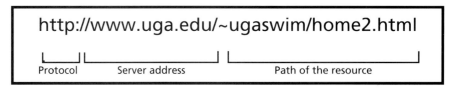

Figure 2-7. Parts of a URL

In computer terminology, a **protocol** is a set of rules that defines how computers will communicate. For Web resources, the protocol (also called the **service resource**) defines the type of resource being retrieved. The Web page resource is defined by the letters **http**, which stands for **Hypertext Transfer Protocol**. In addition to home page documents, some of the other allowable protocols include file, telnet, FTP, and mailto. Table 2-3 shows these protocols (service resources) and their purposes. A very important aspect of these protocols is that they are *all* in lower case, for example, ftp. When included in a URL, the protocols must be entered in this fashion.

Table 2-3: Web protocols

| Protocol | Purpose |
| --- | --- |
| http | Retrieve Web pages |
| file | Retrieve files on local disk |
| telnet | Log onto a computer connected to Internet |
| ftp | Retrieve files from an Internet FTP server |
| mailto | Send outgoing e-mail |
| news | Opens a News program and displays a newsgroup |

The **server address** gives the address of the computer on which the resource is stored. Another name for the server address you will see used is **domain name**. In any case, just as there is a system to city and street addresses and telephone numbers, there is a system for the Internet addresses which is controlled by an organization called the InterNIC Registration Services. A server address is composed of two to five words, separated by periods, that define the name of the server computer (the host), a department or institution, the type of organization, and, possibly, the country of origin. In our example, *www* is the name of the server computer, *uga* is the local institution, and *edu* is the officially registered name that describes the type of organization (educational in this case). The International Standards Organization (ISO) defines the country codes. For example, *us* is the country code for the United States, *au* for Australia, *dk* for Denmark, and *jp* for Japan. These country codes are necessary for all countries other than the United States. Because the Internet originated in the United States, it is not necessary to use the *us* country code. There are six commonly used organizational types shown in Table 2-4.

It is important to note that these Internet addresses are actually an easy-to-remember version of the numeric addresses which computers actually use to communicate. Sometimes you will see these numeric addresses when a Web page is being loaded. However, in general, you do not need to worry about them. When the browser wants to find a particular address, it goes to the **Domain Name Service (DNS),** which is a system that keeps up with all Internet addresses.

Table 2-4: Organization types and identifiers

| Organization type | Identifier |
|---|---|
| educational | edu |
| commercial | com |
| military | mil |
| network | net |
| government | gov |
| generic organizations | org |

The third part of the URL is the **port number,** which indicates an internal address within the server. It is shown as a colon (:) followed by a number immediately after the organization or country code. For example, an address that does have a port number is the URL for the British Broadcasting System.

http://www.bbcnc.org.uk:80/

where the protocol is http, the server name is www.bbcnc.org.uk, and the port number is 80.

The fourth part of the URL is the **path** of the Web resource, which includes the name of the home page file plus any directories or folders in which it is located. In the UGA swim team example, the path of the home page document is ~ugaswim/home2.html. In this case, ~ugaswim is the directory in which the home page file, called home2.html, is stored. The tilde (~) is shorthand for the home directory of the computer on which this file is stored. This is done for security reasons by the person managing the Web server. The extension html refers to the language used to create a home page. For DOS/ Windows 3.1x-based systems, this extension is shortened to htm. Because embedded spaces in path names can create problems, an underscore or dash (e.g., White_House) is used to connect words.

Some other interesting Web site addresses are shown in Table 2-5. Since all URLs describe HTML files, the service component is http in all cases.

Observe in Table 2-5 that some paths end with a slash (e.g., albertos/). This indicates that a **default HTML file,** usually either index.html or default.html, will be accessed. In the case of Alberto's Nightclub, the complete path is interpreted as www.albertos.com/index.html. Use of index or default.html is quite common and saves unnecessary typing. It also means that you can often guess the URL of an organization's home page. For example, you would guess correctly if you tried http://www.dell.com/ to access Dell Computer's home page. Note also that the Rhebokskloof Web page uses *za* as a country code since the winery is located in South Africa.

Once a valid address for a resource has been entered, the next step is automatic: the browser software attempts to connect to the server computer at that address and to find the page referenced in the address. If this operation is successful, then the page is displayed on the screen.

Table 2-5: Interesting Web sites

| URL | Description |
| --- | --- |
| albertos.com/albertos | Alberto's Nightclub in Mountain View, California |
| www.os2.iaccess.za/rhebok/ | Rhebokskloof Estate Winery in South Africa |
| mistral.enst.fr/~pioch/louvre/ | The Louvre Web Site in Paris, France |
| wahoo.netrunner.net/dive/ | ScubaNet.Com Divers Supply |
| key-west.com/margaritaville/ | Jimmy Buffet's Margaritaville |
| unsite.unc.edu/usa/usahome.html | The US home page with on-line information on all 50 states |
| www.mecklerweb.com/mall/ | An Internet Mall with links to many commercial sites |
| www.uml.edu/~ccashman/x-files/x-files.html | THE site for all X-philes |
| ipl.sils.umch.edu/ | The Internet Library with many reference materials |
| www.usatoday.com | An on-line version of *USA Today* |
| www.isworld.org/isworld.html | The best single source on information systems |
| www.career.path.com | A composite of job listings from at least 9 newspapers |
| www.cedar.buffalo.edu/adserv.html | Search for the nine-digit ZIP code for any US address |
| www.whowhere.com | A search engine for information on persons on the Internet |

*Retrieving local files*

One of the shortcomings of the Web is that it takes a great deal of transmission capacity or **bandwidth** on the Internet, especially when graphics, audio, or video files are being transmitted. The bandwidth of the communications lines that connect a computer or local area network to the Internet are measured in bits per second (bps). For example, many institutions are connected to the Internet by T1 lines that transmit approximately 1.5 million bps. However, even lines faster than T1 can be clogged when an entire class attempts to retrieve Web pages at the same time, especially graphic-intensive Web pages. In addition, if everyone in the class simultaneously attempted to access the same Web server, the computer could not handle the demand and very few students would be successful in retrieving a page.

To resolve the problems with inadequate bandwidth and overloaded Web servers, we have created **local files** that have been placed on a hard disk or network file server by your instructor. These local files contain Web pages with graphics just like you would retrieve if you accessed a Web site. To retrieve a Web page stored as a local file on disk, you would use the **file proto-col** instead of the http protocol when entering the URL. The form of the file URL is file:/// plus the local path name. For example, to retrieve the Jimmy Buffett home page from a floppy disk in drive c:, you would enter the URL (If they have been placed on a file server, your instructor will give you the appropriate drive designation.):

file:///c:/weblern2/margarit/index.htm

Note that even though we are working on a Windows system, we have shown the local URL path name with forward slashes (/). However, you can also use backslashes (\) in the path name; Netscape is *smart* enough to allow you to use either front- or backslashes to enter the local URL path name. When we discuss the use of Netscape later in this chapter and in detail in Chapter 3, we will ask you to use the file protocol to retrieve local file Web pages from a hard disk on your local PC. To retrieve the same home page from a Web site, you would simply change the local URL to the appropriate remote URL that uses the http protocol. Note: because Web pages are constantly being changed, the Web pages you retrieve from your hard disk may differ from the same Web pages you retrieve from a Web site. However, they will give you a good look at Web pages without using precious Internet bandwidth.

## Formatting Web pages

It is important to remember that the text displayed on the screen is actually a simple **text (ASCII) file** that contains only keyboard characters and Hypertext Markup Language (HTML) codes. The browser interprets the text and codes to generate the page that appears in the form that you see. This includes retrieving the images and formatting the page to make the text and images to fit the on-screen window. If the window is small, then the text and images will be formatted differently than if the on-screen window is full-screen. Figure 2-8 shows the same UGA swim team Web page shown earlier as Figure 2-4, now reformatted to fit a smaller window. Note that while the text is reformatted, the UGA logo is not reformatted because it is a graphic image.

Another important aspect about browsers and Web pages is that a page will have a very similar appearance when displayed by the same browser on a compatible PC, a Macintosh, or an X-Windows workstation. You do not have to create different versions of a page for the different types of computers currently in use.

## Web page files

Web pages are typically composed of html text files that call other types of files. Most Web pages include some inline graphic or image files that have *gif* or *jpg* extensions that are automatically loaded with the Web page. The text portion of the page is retrieved fairly quickly, but the image files that are linked to the page can take some time to be received from the server. This can especially be true if the page is being received over a modem. For this reason, most browsers offer the capability to only display text, ignoring images when a page is being retrieved or to allow the user to scroll down a page and read text elements even while the images are still being received. That way, users do not have to wait for images to be completely received before reading the textual information on the page.

Figure 2-8. Page reformatted in a smaller window

In addition to the html and small image files that are integral parts of Web pages, many other types of files can also be linked to a Web page. These include large images as well as audio, video, animation, and even three-dimensional image files. While text and small images are automatically displayed by the browser when the page is retrieved, the other types of files need an additional program called a **helper application** to be played or displayed. These helper applications are linked to the browser in such a way that they are invoked automatically when the user requests an audio or video file or a large image. Helper applications are also launched when Netscape recognizes the type of file that is being downloaded. For example, if you use Netscape to download a presentation software file with a PowerPoint (ppt) extension, Netscape will automatically launch the PowerPoint viewer.

With the Introduction of Netscape 2.0, Netscape introduced the concept of plug-in applications. A **plug-in** is a program that can seamlessly handle some file type within Netscape. Ideally, a plug-in adds features to a main program in such a way that the new capabilities seem to be part of the original program. An example of this is the RealAudio[4] plug-in which enables Netscape to play *streaming audio,* that is, sound at the same time as it is being sent to your computer over the Internet. Prior to the introduction of plug-ins like RealAudio, it was necessary to download an entire audio file with a *wav* or *au* extension and then play it using a helper application. Other plug-ins enable Netscape users to use outside software applications and to view video files, animation, and 3-D images. For example, a popular plug-in that enables you to view animation and video files is Shockwave.[5]

You should be aware that attempting to use a plug-in to carry out these operations with a modem can be a frustrating process. Even with the fastest modem which transfers data at a maximum rate of 33,600 bps, the quality of audio played by RealAudio is often equivalent to listening to a distant radio station, and the sound can be lost for several seconds at a time. Similarly, viewing video files over a modem is a very slow process since they require so much bandwidth.

## Other browser operations

Once a home or other Web page has been retrieved, you can then use a browser to perform other operations including: linking to other Web pages, navigating among them, retrieving previously viewed Web pages, searching for interesting Web pages, saving and printing Web pages, filling out forms, and using maps in a Web page.

### Linking to other Web pages

You may link to other Web pages from the current page by simply clicking on a hypertext link. Recall that these can be underlined words or phrases or highlighted graphics or images. When you click on the hypertext link, the associated Web page is automatically retrieved (assuming a connection can be made to the Web server).

### Navigating among Web pages

Once you have linked to another Web page from the home page, you can begin navigating among Web pages. Browsers automatically keep up with the URLs of Web pages that have been visited. There are reverse and forward buttons that allow you to move backward and forward through previously visited home pages. There is a history option that will store a partial list of recently visited Web site URLs. You can select a URL from the history list and jump to that page. Finally, there is a home button that sends you back to the *home* Web site that automatically appears on the screen when the browser is accessed.

---

4. http://www.realaudio.com/
5. http://www.macromedia.com/shockwave/plugin/

*Remember-
ing home
page
addresses*

Once you have found an interesting Web page, browsers can help you remember its URL. They do this via an operation called *Bookmarks*. If a URL is saved to a Bookmarks file, it can then be accessed without reentry. For example, you could save the ScubaNet URL in a Bookmarks file and then later select it or some other URL that has been saved. This is true regardless of whether the Web page is retrieved from a Web site or as a local file from disk. While it might seem that Bookmarks and history lists are the same, they are actually quite different. The Bookmarks list is a *static* list that does not change unless you add another bookmark or remove an existing one. Otherwise, it will stay the same from session to session. On the other hand, the history list is *dynamic,* changing as you move around Web pages, and disappears when you exit the browser.

*Searching
for Web
pages*

As more and more people and organizations place information on the Web, finding this information is becoming an important operation. With millions and millions of Web pages available, without a search mechanism, you could spend hours searching for the appropriate information. Searching for information on the Web involves defining some criteria to direct the search. In every case, the browser is not doing the actual searching, but is utilizing one of several **search engines** that have been developed for Web users. These search engines go by such names as Alta Vista[6], InfoSeek Guide[7], and Yahoo![8]. Regardless of the name, all of these search programs allow you to enter a word or phrase that is used to search for matching Web pages and Newsgroup messages. With an appropriate search, you can often find a wealth of information on virtually any subject. The searching process will be discussed in more detail in Chapters 3 and 5.

*Saving or
printing
retrieved
information*

Once a Web page has been displayed, all or part of it may be saved to a local file under the page file name or under a name you assign. For example, if you saved the ScubaNet home page on a Windows system, it would be saved on your local disk as index.htm or another name you choose. You can also print this page.

   If you choose to save the page to a local file, it is important to remember that the images will *not* be automatically saved along with the Web page text. Since they are separate files, they must be saved separately. This means that if you bring the local file into the browser, you will see only the text. In many cases, however, the text by itself can be very useful to you since it contains much important information as well as all of the hypertext links to other documents. If you retrieved a saved Web page using the file protocol, you would only see the text with no images.

_____

6. http://altavista.digital.com/

7. http://guide.infoseek.com/

8. http://www.yahoo.com/search.html

Another important aspect of a saved Web page file is that if it is retrieved into an editor like WordPad or Notepad, you will see the text version with the HTML tags. Recall that these tags are interpreted by the browser to format the page by generating the styles and sizes of text, provide links to other documents, and retrieve the image, audio, and video files. By studying these saved Web pages, you can learn a great deal that will help you when you develop your own Web page. Figure 2-9 shows a portion of the UGA swim team home page in text form. You can pick out the HTML tags since they are all enclosed in *less than* (<) and *greater-than* (>) signs. For example, the title of the home page, "Welcome-The UGA Swimming and Diving Team," is surrounded by the HTML title tags (<title> and </title>.) These tags and their usage are discussed in detail in Chapter 4.

```
Netscape - [Source of: http://www.uga.edu/~ugaswim/home2.html]          _ 🗗 ✕

<html>
<head>
<script language="JavaScript">

<!--Hiding from non-conpliant browsers
function ncaa() {
      alert ("NCAA 200 Free Relay Champs");
}

// End hiding-->

</script>
<title>Welcome - The UGA Swimming and Diving Team</title>
</head>
<body bgcolor="ffffff" text="000000" link="ff0000" vlink="646060"><strong>
```

Figure 2-9. UGA swim team home page in text form

You may also choose to print the current Web page. When this is done, the page is printed exactly as it is displayed on the screen, including all graphics. This *What You See Is What You Get (WYSIWYG)* printing capability of Web browsers is an important feature that allows users to obtain printed versions of Web pages. Figure 2-10 shows a portion of the printed version of the UGA swim team home page. Note that it looks very much like the swim team home page displayed in Figure 2-4. In fact, the only differences are that not all of the printed Web page can be displayed on the screen and that, unless you are using a color printer, the page will be printed in black and white.

*Forms, e-mail, and clickable maps*

Three very useful features of Web pages are forms, e-mail, and clickable maps. E-mail and forms are critical to the successful use of the Internet and Web for electronic commerce while, maps are a way of using parts of a graphic image as hypertext links.

For the Internet and Web to be successful avenues for electronic commerce, there must be a way for customers to send information back to the company or to order products electronically. **Forms** provide this capability by allowing the user to fill out information and submit it to the company's Web server where it is interpreted by software on the server. To order a product or

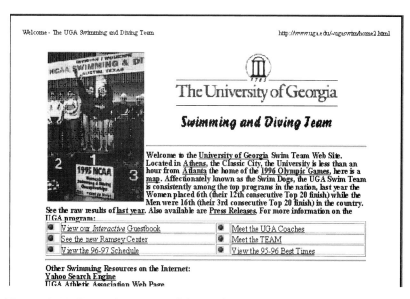

Figure 2-10. Printed version of the Web page

request more information about a product, the user simply fills out a form and clicks on *Submit* or *Send*. Forms are becoming very sophisticated, with passwords being required to access some forms and others being used to enable people to join clubs and buying groups. Figure 2-11 shows a form used for ordering items from Jimmy Buffett's Margaritaville Store in Key West, Florida.

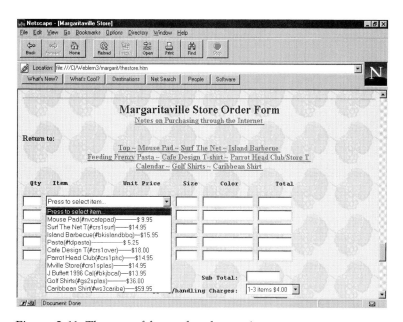

Figure 2-11. The use of forms for electronic commerce

The only problem with using forms to facilitate electronic commerce is protecting sensitive information like credit card numbers from being stolen while the form is making its way back to the Web server. However, there are now **secure servers** that provide this protection. Security is discussed in more detail in Chapter 6.

In early versions of Navigator, you could send but not receive e-mail over the Web. However, starting with Navigator version 2.0, it is now possible to also receive e-mail. In addition to using forms to accept orders and other information from users, most commercial Web sites also use the mailto protocol to provide a hypertext link to their e-mail. This process is very easy, requiring only that you click the hypertext link and fill in the text of the message. Figure 2-12 shows how individuals who visit the Margaritaville Web page can use the mailto protocol to send messages to the page's creators.

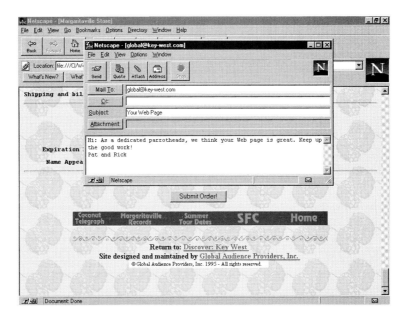

Figure 2-12. Use of return e-mail

With the introduction of Navigator 2.0, outgoing e-mail capability was added. This built-in e-mail client works like most other e-mail software; you can send and receive e-mail by using the menu system or the mail client. The Navigator e-mail client will be discussed in more detail in Chapter 5.

A **clickable map** is a graphical image on which sections act as hypertext links to other Web pages. Instead of clicking on a highlighted word or phrase to retrieve a Web page, you click on a portion of the map. Figure 2-13 shows a clickable map from the Margaritaville Store home page. In this example, the clickable map is in the form of a menu bar from which you can access any of the five options by clicking on the appropriate area. Like forms and e-mail, clickable maps depend on Internet access and a Web server computer to interpret the results, so they cannot be used in a local mode.

Figure 2-13. Clickable map

## Introduction to Netscape Navigator

As we mentioned earlier, Netscape Navigator is the most popular browser in use today. In some surveys, up to 80 percent of all persons on the Web use the Netscape browser. In this section, we will introduce you to Netscape by showing you how to access it, retrieve a home page from disk, and then move back and forth to other related Web pages. In Chapter 3, we will provide a detailed discussion of Netscape.

### Accessing Netscape

Since we assume you are using either Windows 3.x or Windows 95 to access the Netscape browser, accessing Netscape is very easy: simply find the Netscape icon on the desktop and double click it. (If there is a Netscape program group icon, double click it first.) The Netscape icon will either be a square with a capital N on a background showing the curvature of the earth (Netscape 1.x) or a ship's wheel (Netscape 2.x or 3.x). Figure 2-14 shows the Windows icon for Netscape 3.0.

Figure 2-14. The Netscape icon

### Netscape screen

After you have accessed Netscape, the Netscape screen appears. The format of this screen is essentially the same regardless of whether you are using Windows 3.x, Windows 95, or the Macintosh, so these instructions will be the same regardless of the system. The contents of the screen, however, will differ depending on how your network manager or instructor has configured your system. The screen may come up blank, or it may contain a home page that is automatically loaded when Netscape is accessed. This *home* location might be the Netscape corporate home page or some other Web site if your system is connected to the Internet and has sufficient bandwidth. On the other hand, we have created a *home* site with information on this textbook that is stored on your floppy disk under the URL

file:///c:/weblern2/webbook.htm

This local file *home* site is shown in Figure 2-15.

Note in Figure 2-15 that the URL for this home page is shown in the location box. Observe that there are a series of menu options at the top of the screen beginning with File and ending with Help. There are also two rows of buttons above and below a text box in which the address of the current Web site is displayed. In this chapter, we will have you click on a link to retrieve another Web page that is stored on your disk.

41

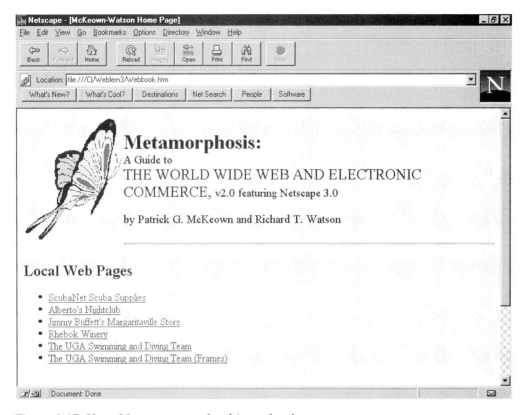

Figure 2-15. *Home* Netscape page for this textbook

## Your Turn!

1. If you are not already in Windows (or the Macintosh operating system), access it as directed by your instructor.

2. Access Netscape as discussed above. The home page shown in Figure 2-15 should be displayed. If it is not displayed, then click the Open button and enter file:///weblern2/webbook.htm.

3. Point out the browser elements, that is, menu bar, buttons, Web page address, main screen, hypertext links, and graphics, on the Netscape screen.

| | |
|---|---|
| *Using a hypertext link to retrieve a Web page* | As an example of using a hypertext link in Netscape to retrieve a Web page, we will use the home page for this textbook shown in Figure 2-15, which has links to the Web pages for the four companies we discussed in Chapter 1— ScubaNet, Alberto's, the Rhebokskloof Winery, and Jimmy Buffett's Margaritaville Store. In this case, we will retrieve the ScubaNet home page shown earlier by clicking on that link in the textbook home page. When this is done, the ScubaNet home page shown in Figure 2-3 is displayed in Netscape. |

## Your Turn!

1. Place the pointer over an underlined link to the ScubaNet home page (<u>ScubaNet Scuba Supplies</u>). Note that the pointer changes to a pointing finger. Notice also that the local URL for the ScubaNet home page
   file:///c:/weblern2/scubanet/index.htm
   is shown in the bottom line of the Netscape browser.

2. Single-click on the underlined link to the ScubaNet home page. You should see the same Web page shown earlier as Figure 2-3.

| | |
|---|---|
| *Navigating to other Web pages* | In looking at the ScubaNet home page on your screen, you will note that there are a new set of links to associated Web pages. If you click on any of the graphics with red borders, a related Web page will be retrieved and displayed. For example, if you click on Diveflag Swimsuit box, the Web page shown earlier in Figure 1-7 will be displayed. |

You may go back to the home page by clicking on <u>Back to Home Page</u> at the bottom of this page or by clicking the Back toolbar button. You may then return to the Swimsuit page by clicking on the Forward toolbar button. If, at any time, the process of retrieving a Web page seems to be delayed (no action on the screen or a partial retrieval) you may stop the retrieval process by clicking on the Stop toolbar button and then click on the hypertext link again.

## Your turn!

1. Click on the Diveflag Swimsuit link in the ScubaNet home page to retrieve the swimsuit page. It should look like Figure 1-7.

2. Click on Back to return to the home page. Click on Forward to return to the swimsuit Web page. Click on the <u>Back to Home Page</u> hypertext link at the bottom of the page to return to the ScubaNet home page.

3. Now retrieve the "This Month's Special Regulator" link to retrieve the corresponding Web page. Now click on Home to return to the textbook home page.

*Exiting Netscape*

Now that you have had a quick tour of Netscape, you can exit the browser by clicking on File and clicking on the Exit option from the resulting pull-down menu. You may also exit Netscape by double-clicking on the Control Menu box.

## Key terms and concepts

bandwidth
browser
clickable map
client/server network
content area
default HTML file
directory buttons
domain name
domain name service (DNS)
e-mail
file protocol
file transfer protocol (FTP)
form
graphic elements
helper application
home page
hypermedia
hypertext
hypertext link
hypertext markup language (HTML)
hypertext transfer protocol (http)
local file
location window

menu bar
mouse pointer
multimedia
newsgroup (news)
path
plug-in
port number
protocol
scroll bars
search engine
secure server
server address
service resource
telnet
text (ASCII) file
title bar
toolbar buttons
uniform resource locator (URL)
Web page
Web page address
Web site

## Exercises

1. What are the key elements of a Web browser? What is *hypermedia?*

2. What difficulties in using the Internet are discussed in the text? How do Web browsers resolve these problems?

3. What are the four primary Internet applications in addition to the Web?

4. What was the nature of the first Web browsers? How do current browsers differ from the original browsers?

5. What is a Web page? What is a home page? Are all Web pages also home pages? Why or why not?

6. What are the primary elements of a browser? What is a *clickable link*?

7. List and briefly discuss each of the key browser operations. Describe the reformatting operation.

8. What are the parts of a URL? List five protocols and their purpose. What is the purpose of a default HTML file?

9. Why do we ask you to retrieve local files rather than retrieving them from the Internet? What does bandwidth have to do with this?

10. Why are helper software packages needed? What are plug-ins?

11. What are Bookmarks? What browser operations do they facilitate?

12. What are forms used for? How are they related to business use of the Web? Why are secure servers needed? Why can't you use forms in local mode?

13. Access Netscape using Windows 3.1 or Windows 95 (or the Macintosh). From the *home* Web page that appears when you access Netscape, click on Jimmy Buffet's Margaritaville to view Jimmy Buffett's Margaritaville home page. Scroll down the page and click on the map. Does it work in local mode? Why not? Click on the Margaritaville Store link to view the items for sale and the form that is used to order them. Go back to the Margaritaville home page and go to the last two lines. Click on MARGARITAVILLE to display the outgoing mail message screen. Note the e-mail address and then click on cancel. Click on the Back button to return to the textbook home page.

14. Click on Rhebok Winery to view the home page for the Rhebok Winery in South Africa. Scroll down this page and click on the Place an Order link. View the items for sale and the form that is used to order them. Click on the Home button to return to the textbook home page.

15. Click on Alberto's Nightclub to view Alberto's Nightclub home page. Click on File from the menu bar, then click on Exit to exit Netscape.

# 3    Using Netscape

- - - - - - - - - - - - - - - - - - - - - - - - - - - - - - - - - - -

**Objectives**

After completing this chapter, you will be able to:

❖ discuss the use of the Netscape Navigator browser to navigate the World Wide Web;

❖ access Netscape on your system and describe specific elements of Netscape;

❖ use the Netscape toolbar buttons to carry out important browser operations;

❖ use the menu bar to carry out the same operations as the toolbar in addition to handling other important operations;

❖ control the appearance of the Netscape screen and change various default settings;

❖ discuss the use of the Directory buttons to carry out a variety of special operations;

❖ understand the use of frames in Web pages;

❖ work popup menus to navigate within Web sites and save images to disk.

**Introduction**

As with other Web browsers, the primary purpose of Netscape Navigator is to access the ever growing number of Web sites. In this chapter, we will briefly review accessing Netscape and then discuss special elements not mentioned earlier. We will then discuss in detail how to use Netscape to perform the key browser operations listed in Chapter 2. We will also discuss other operations that can be accomplished with Netscape. Throughout this discussion, you will note that there are usually two or more ways

to carry out most operations. You can use a menu option to perform an operation or use one of the two sets of buttons located beneath the menu bar to do
the same thing. For example, there are three ways to enter the URL of a Web
page: use a button, use a menu option, or enter the URL directly in the location box. As you become familiar with Netscape, you may find that you favor
one method over another. You should use the one most comfortable to you.

*Accessing*
*Netscape*

Since we assume you are using either Windows 3.x or Windows 95 to access
the Netscape browser, accessing Netscape is very easy: simply find the
Netscape icon on the desktop and double click it. (If there is a Netscape program group icon, double click it first.) The Netscape icon will either be a
square with a capital N on a background showing the curvature of the earth
(Netscape 1.x) or a ship's wheel (Netscape 2.x or 3.x). After you double click
on the Netscape icon, the opening home page is displayed as shown in Figure
3-1. Recall that the **opening home page** is a Web page loaded when you
access Netscape. In this case, the opening home page contains information
about this textbook plus links to other Web pages.[1]

In looking at the home page in Figure 3-1, three elements at the bottom of
the Netscape screen should be noted in more detail than was given in Chapter
2. These are the security area, the progress bar, and the mail indicator. In the
bottom left-hand corner of the Netscape screen is the **security area,** which displays a door key. If the door key is displayed unbroken on a blue background,
then the home page is considered secure—that is, it is less susceptible to fraud
and other misuse by hackers or other electronic criminals. This is an
extremely important issue for companies that are interested in doing business
on the Web. They must be able to send and receive information over the Internet with the knowledge that no one can eavesdrop on the message, copy it, or
otherwise damage the contents. A secure Web page means that users can send
credit card numbers over the Web without having to worry about it being
intercepted by a hacker. If the door key is shown broken on a grey background, then the home page is insecure and there is no guarantee that information will not be stolen, copied, or damaged. Security will be discussed in
more detail in Chapter 6.

At the bottom center of the Netscape window is the **progress bar** that
uses both text and graphics to display the status of loading a Web page as
well as other useful information. On the right-hand side of the progress bar is
a graphical bar that shows the amount of the Web page that has been loaded.
When loading is complete, the graphic progress bar disappears. On the left-
hand side of the progress bar is text that provides a variety of information
regarding the Web page being loaded. For example, when the pointer is positioned over a hypertext link, the text portion of the progress bar displays the
corresponding URL. The text portion also shows the URL of each file that is
being loaded and the status of the loading process in terms of bytes of infor-

1. If it is not displayed, then click the Open button and enter
file:///weblern2/webbook.htm.

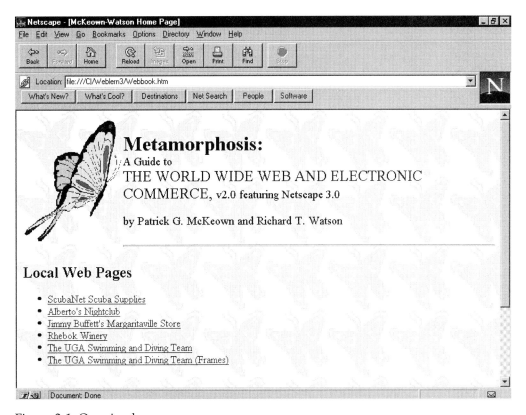

Figure 3-1. Opening home page

mation loaded relative to the total number of bytes in the file. When the process is completed, the progress bar will display the message "Document: Done." Table 3-1 shows various messages which you may see in the progress bar along with their meaning.

At the bottom right-hand corner of the screen is the **mail indicator.** There is always a picture of an envelope in this location, and there may be either a question mark or an exclamation mark. The question mark indicates you have not yet checked your mail during this Web session, and the exclamation mark indicates you have unread mail. Clicking the envelope takes you to the integrated Netscape e-mail client in which you can perform a variety of e-mail related activities. The e-mail client will be discussed further in Chapter 5.

## Your turn!

1. Access Netscape from your PC. What is the URL of the starting home page that loads automatically when you access Netscape?

Table 3-1: Progress bar messages

| Progress bar message | Meaning of message |
|---|---|
| Connect: Looking up host: www.negia.net | Netscape is looking up the host address part of the URL to find the Web server |
| Connect: Contacting host: www.negia.net | Netscape has sent a message to the server computer and is waiting for an acknowledgment that the message has been received |
| Connect: Host Contacted: Waiting for reply | Netscape has sent a message to the server and is waiting for a reply |
| Transferring data | Server computer has begun sending the Web page to the local computer |
| 45% of 80K | Messages similar to this one indicate how much of the document has been sent |
| Document: Done | The entire document has been received |
| Unable to locate host: www.negia.net | Netscape cannot find the host computer in the Domain Name Service (DNS). You will also see a dialog box saying, "The server does not have a DNS entry." Check the address and correct any errors. Otherwise, you may assume the server no longer exists. |
| Interrupt the current transfer | There is a problem with the transfer. You should probably try again. |

2. Once the opening home page for this textbook is on-screen, point out the parts of the Netscape window. If this page is not on the screen, position the mouse pointer over the Home toolbar button and click the left mouse button *once*.

3. Position the mouse pointer over the Open toolbar button and click the left mouse button *once*. Press the Escape (Esc) key to cancel this operation.

4. Position the pointer on the ScubaNet link and note the URL of this Web page in the progress bar. Do the same for the Alberto's home page.

------------------------------------------------

## Versions of Netscape

Since its first introduction in the Fall of 1994, Netscape Navigator has gone through a series of versions, with each version adding new features or correcting problems with previous versions. The versions in most widespread use today are Netscape Navigator 1.x, 2.x, and 3.x. Version 4.0 is scheduled to be released in early 1997. Netscape 2.0 added the capability to receive as well as send e-mail and to upload FTP files. It also added integrated newsgroups (News), a new type of bookmark operation, and a new feature called *frames* which enable you to see two or more Web pages simultaneously. Netscape 2.0 also included for the first time the capability to integrate plug-in programs that extended its multimedia capabilities as well as the capability to run programs that are included in the Web page without having to return to the Web server. These programs are written in either the Java or JavaScript languages.

Netscape Navigator 3.0 incorporated many elements that previously had to be run as separate plug-in programs. These included listening to audio and watching video directly from Web pages, working with three-dimensional Web pages, and using the Internet as a long distance phone tool. However, as with many other software packages, each subsequent version of Netscape Navigator has been larger and has required more disk space and internal memory to run as Netscape has responded to competition from Microsoft by adding more features to the basic browser. Due to the popularity of Netscape 3.x, we have chosen to concentrate on it in this text. To determine which version of Netscape you are using, you can click on Help on the menu bar and then click on About Netscape.

The most obvious difference between the three versions of Netscape in common use are the Directory buttons. All three versions have What's New, What's Cool, and Net Search buttons, but they differ after these three. In any case, the Directory buttons enable you to quickly link to useful and interesting Web pages. The Directory buttons will be discussed in detail in Chapter 5. Another difference between Netscape 1.x and 2.x or 3.x is that an additional menu bar option, the Window option, has been added in the later versions. Like other menu options, it will be discussed later in this chapter.

## Using local files

As we discussed in Chapter 2, a variety of local Web page files associated with this textbook are available to you. To avoid the problems that can be encountered when a group of students all try to access the same Web site on the Internet, we will ask that you access these local Web pages. The process of accessing a local home page and one on the Web is exactly the same with one exception: a different URL. The URL for a Web page is composed of **http://** plus the Web server name and the path name of the Web page. On the other hand, the URL for a local file is composed of **file:///** plus the path of the Web page file (including the drive letter). For example, the URL for the ScubaNet home page on the Internet is

http://wahoo.netrunner.net/dive/

The URL for the same home page stored on hard disk is:

file:///c:/weblern2/scubanet/index.htm

When you use the file:/// protocol to retrieve one of the local Web sites we have provided your instructor, you and your fellow students can all access the *same* Web site without encountering any delay due to the Internet being slow or the Web server being overloaded. The text and graphics will load quickly and, at the same time, you are not using up any Internet bandwidth.[2]

---

2. You may download the file that creates these files by visiting the support Web page for this textbook at http://www.negia.net/webbook. Follow the instructions given there to create these local Web pages on your PC.

■ ━ ■ ━ ■ ━ ■ ━ ■ ■ ━ ■ ■ ━ ■ ■ ━ ■ ■ ━ ■ ■ ━ ■ ■

## Your turn!

1. Which version of Netscape Navigator are you using? What Directory buttons do you have in addition to the three mentioned in the text?

2. Why do we suggest using local files to learn about Netscape? What protocol should you use to retrieve a local Web page?

■ ━ ■ ■ ━ ■ ━ ■ ■ ━ ■ ■ ■ ■ ■ ■ ■ ■ ■ ■ ■ ■ ■ ━ ■ ■ ━ ■

## Working with Web pages

Now that you know the elements of the Netscape window, you are ready to use Netscape to navigate the Web. In this chapter, we will discuss using Netscape to carry out several operations on the Web, including:

❖ retrieving a home page;

❖ linking to other Web pages;

❖ navigating among Web pages;

❖ retrieving previously viewed Web pages;

❖ saving and printing Web pages;
  Other Netscape operations will be covered in subsequent chapters.

## *Point and click naviga- tion*

One of the valuable features of Netscape and other graphical browsers is **point and click navigation**, in which you use your mouse or other pointing device to position the **mouse pointer** over the hypertext links or the menu bar, toolbar, location window, or directory buttons. You can then click a mouse button to execute the corresponding command. The mouse pointer changes shape in Netscape depending on where it is positioned. Usually, the Netscape pointer is an arrow and, if the pointer is positioned over a menu item or button and the left mouse button clicked, the corresponding menu item or button will be selected. You can also position the mouse pointer on the scroll bar to move up and down through the Web page. If the pointer is positioned over the location window, it changes to a vertical line, which allows you to delete an existing URL and enter a new one into the location window. When positioned over a hypertext link, the pointer changes to a hand with pointing finger, and if you click the left mouse button, the corresponding Web page will be retrieved. Finally, when a Web page is being retrieved, the mouse pointer will change to an hourglass indicating that you must wait for the page to be loaded. It is important to note that in *all* cases involving making a selection with the Netscape pointer, you only need to click the mouse button *once*, not twice as with many Windows operations. Table 3-2 shows the various shapes of the mouse pointer in Netscape and the associated actions.

Table 3-2: Mouse pointer shapes in Netscape

| Shape | When used? | Actions |
|---|---|---|
| Arrowhead | Always unless positioned over hypertext link or location window or waiting for page to load | Select from menus, toolbar, and directory buttons, and scroll up and down Web page |
| Vertical line | When positioned in location window | Delete existing Web address and enter address of new page to retrieve |
| Pointing finger | When positioned over hypertext link | Retrieve associated Web page |
| Hour glass | When waiting for a Web page to load | Wait! |

## Your turn!

1. Move the pointer to the Alberto's Nightclub hypertext link on the textbook home page. What is the shape of the pointer? Now click the left mouse button to retrieve this page.

2. Move the pointer to the location window. What is the shape of the pointer? Now click the left mouse button and then delete the existing URL.

3. Enter the URL for the textbook home page, that is,
   file:///c:/weblern2/webbook.htm
   in the location window and press Enter. You should now be back at the textbook home page.

*Using the toolbar*

The easiest way to navigate the Web and work with Web pages is to use the **toolbar**. Recall that the toolbar is located immediately beneath the menu bar and contains nine buttons. To use a toolbar button, simply position the pointer over the button and click the left mouse button. Figure 3-2 shows the Netscape toolbar.

Figure 3-2. Netscape toolbar

The nine buttons on the toolbar are divided into three groups: navigation, file operations, and stop. The navigation buttons allow you to move around previously retrieved home pages, while the file operations buttons carry out various operations with the Web page files, including opening and printing them. The Stop button cancels the loading process whenever the process takes too long or you decide not to complete retrieval. Table 3-3 lists the nine tool-bar buttons along with their groups and purpose. We have also shown the shortcut key combinations that can be used instead of clicking a button. **Shortcut keys** often use the Ctrl key in conjunction with a letter. For example, you can select the Open option directly by pressing Ctrl-L instead of clicking on the toolbar Open button. If you are using a special version of Netscape called *Netscape Gold* that combines Netscape Navigator with a Web page creation program, you will see an additional button–the *Edit Button*–which is used to help create Web pages. You may ignore this button for the time being, but it will be discussed in Chapter 4.

Table 3-3: Toolbar buttons

| Button | Group | Purpose | Windows shortcut key |
|---|---|---|---|
| Back | Navigation | Move backward to a previous page | Ctrl + Left Arrow |
| Forward | Navigation | Move forward to a previous page | Ctrl + Right Arrow |
| Home | Navigation | Move to page that is retrieved when Netscape is accessed | None |
| Reload | File Operation | Start the retrieval process again (used when a page is corrupted during display) | Ctrl + R |
| Images | File Operation | Load images if they were not loaded with the text | Ctrl + I |
| Open | File Operation | Display Open Location dialog box for entry of URL | Ctrl + L |
| Print | File Operation | Print the currently displayed page | None |
| Find | File Operation | Look for a word or phrase in the *currently* displayed page (does *not* search for home pages) | Ctrl + F |
| Stop | Stop | Terminate the retrieval of a page (used if transfer process is too slow) | Esc (Escape) |

As an example of a file operation to retrieve a Web page, you would simply click on the Open button to display the Open Location dialog box as shown in Figure 3-3 and enter the URL for the desired Web page.

When a remote Web page with an http protocol is retrieved through either a hypertext link or by entering a URL in the location box or in the Open Location dialog box, the browser goes through four steps:

1. looking for the server with the address shown in this URL;
2. connecting to the server;
3. waiting for a reply;
4. transferring the Web page file to the user's machine.

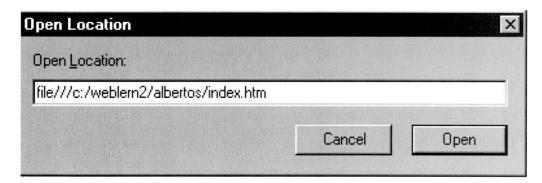

Figure 3-3. Open location dialog box

During this process, the progress bar at the bottom of the screen shows the status of the retrieval. Note that when a local Web page with a file protocol is retrieved, the page is retrieved from a hard disk and displayed on the screen after going through the first three steps.

To navigate among Web pages, you can use the Back, Forward, and Home toolbar buttons. The Back button returns you to a previously viewed Web page and the Forward button goes *forward* through a series of previously viewed Web pages. The Home button automatically retrieves the opening home page. The location of this Web page is usually defined by the person installing Netscape and can be a local page or a page somewhere on the Internet.

## Your turn!

1. From the textbook home page, click on the ScubaNet hypertext link. Now, click on the Open button and enter the following URL:
   file:///c:/weblern2/albertos/index.htm
   to retrieve the local Web page for Alberto's Night Club.

2. Click on the Back button to return to the previous (ScubaNet) Web page.

3. Click on the Forward button to return to the Alberto's home page.

4. Click on the Home button to return to the textbook home page that was originally loaded when you accessed Netscape.

*Other tool-bar buttons*

In addition to the Open button and the three navigation buttons, there are five other buttons. To print the currently displayed Web page, you can use the print Button. This will display the Windows Print dialog window in which you can click OK to activate printing or click Cancel to cancel the process.

To search for a word or phrase in the Web page, you can click on Find to display the Find dialog box in which you enter the word or phrase. This is *not* the same as searching for a Web page on a particular topic. It is like the *find* operation available in word processing software. For example, to search for the word *order* in the ScubaNet home page, you would click on the Find button and then fill in the dialog box. When this is done, the word or phrase is highlighted in the Web page.

The Reload toolbar button is used to request that a Web page be retrieved again. The Reload process is necessary if the Web page is somehow corrupted during transmission over the Internet. Graphics may be only partially displayed or text can be *garbage* or conflict with images. If this occurs, then clicking on Reload automatically retrieves the current Web page. Netscape keeps both a memory cache and a disk cache. A **memory cache** is a copy of recent Web pages in computer memory, and a **disk cache** is a larger number of recently visited Web pages stored on disk. This means that recently visited Web pages can be reloaded more quickly from memory or disk than from a distant Web site.

It is possible to set up Netscape so only the text of a Web page will be retrieved without images. This may be done if the Web page is being retrieved over a modem or if the connection to the server is slow due to heavy traffic. If you then decide that you wish to view the missing images, click on the Images toolbar button. Figure 3-4 shows the ScubaNet home page without images and after the Image button is clicked.

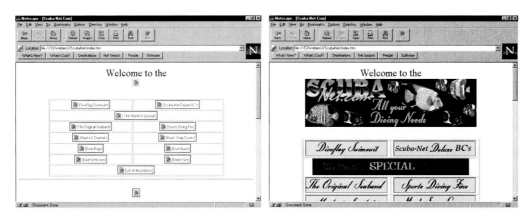

Figure 3-4. Web page without and with images

Finally, the Stop button terminates the retrieval process. Slow retrieval of a Web page is seldom a problem when retrieving local Web page files, but it can be an obvious one when retrieving a remote Web page that contains many images, or very large images over the Internet. This is especially true when you are retrieving Web pages over a modem.

------------------------------------------------

## Your turn!

1. Use the toolbar's Home button to retrieve the textbook home page and then use the toolbar Print button to print it. (Check with your instructor before beginning this process.)

2. Click on the toolbar's Find button, enter the word *Web*, and press Enter. You should now see the word *Web* highlighted in the textbook home page. Press Esc to cancel the Find process.

3. Click on the toolbar's Reload button to retrieve the textbook home page again.

------------------------------------------------

## About the menu bar

So far, we have covered the use of the mouse pointer and toolbar buttons to handle two of the browser operations listed earlier (retrieving a Web page and linking to other Web pages) and parts of two other operations (navigating among Web pages and printing a Web page). To accomplish the remaining browser operations, you must use the **menu bar**.

As discussed previously, *all* of the necessary commands in Netscape can be accomplished by the nine menu bar options: File, Edit, View, Go, Bookmarks, Options, Window, Directory, and Help. This includes the toolbar button operations just discussed. Each of these menu bar options has a submenu from which you then select the actual command. The menu bar is shown in Figure 3-5. (If you are using Netscape 1.x, you will not have the Window menu bar option.)

| File  Edit  View  Go  Bookmarks  Options  Directory  Window  Help |
|---|

Figure 3-5. Netscape menu bar

### Overview of menu options

There are eight options on the menu bar summarized in Table 3-4. Note that the first six options involve actual commands that affect the operation of Netscape, while the last two retrieve home pages to your screen that provide you with interesting information or help in using Netscape. Since the home pages listed in the Directory and Help submenus require access to the Web over the Internet, we suggest that you *not* select any of these home pages unless told to do so.

You may select an option from the menu bar in a variety of ways, but in this text we will assume you will use the mouse to position the mouse pointer over the desired option and click the left mouse button once. For example, to select the File option from the menu bar, you would position the mouse pointer (an arrow) over the File option and single click the left mouse button. Once the menu bar File option has been selected, a submenu appears as shown in Figure 3-6. In any case, you can cancel the option selection by either

Table 3-4: Menu option command summary

| Menu option | Command summary |
|---|---|
| File | Opens or closes URLs or local files, saves or prints home page, sends e-mail, or exits Netscape |
| Edit | Enables copying of portions of home pages or finding words or phrases in a home page |
| View | Controls loading of home page and images |
| Go | Enables navigation between home pages and shows history of current Netscape session |
| Bookmarks | Lists previously saved URLs of home pages and enables saving the current URL |
| Options | Controls the appearance of Netscape screen and other settings |
| Directory | Lists interesting and useful home pages |
| Window | Provides access to e-mail, News, Address Book, Bookmarks, and the history list |
| Help | Provides a variety of help tools including an on-line handbook and reference source |

pressing the Esc (Escape) key or by moving the mouse pointer off the submenu and clicking the left mouse button.

## Your turn!

1. Access the File option on the menu bar. Compare the drop down menu you see with that in Figure 3-6. Press the Escape (Esc) key to cancel this operation.

2. Select the View menu bar option and note the commands listed in the drop down menu.

3. Select the Options menu bar option and note which of the commands are checked. If the Show Toolbar command is checked, click on it. What happens to the Netscape screen? Now click on this selection again and note the result.

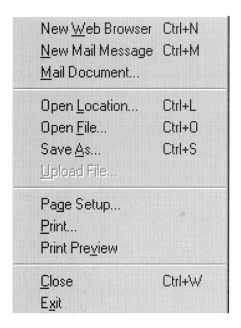

Figure 3-6. File drop down submenu

**Executing menu commands**

Once you have a drop down submenu for a menu bar option, you can select from it in a variety of ways, but, once again, we will assume you will use your mouse to position the pointer over the command and click the left mouse button once. For example, if you selected the File menu option as discussed previously, you can then select the Open Location option by clicking on it.

Note in Figure 3-6 that six of the submenu options have shortcut keys associated with them. As with the toolbar buttons, you can bypass the menu bar and activate these file submenu options directly by using the shortcut keys.

■ ■ ■ ■ ■ ■ ■ ■ ■ ■ ■ ■ ■ ■ ■ ■ ■ ■ ■ ■ ■ ■ ■

## Your turn!

1. Access the File option from the menu bar and highlight Open Location to select this command from the drop down menu. Press Esc to cancel this operation.

■ ■ ■ ■ ■ ■ ■ ■ ■ ■ ■ ■ ■ ■ ■ ■ ■ ■ ■ ■ ■ ■ ■

**Using the menu bar options**

In this section, we will discuss each of the nine menu bar options and the corresponding submenus in some detail. In several instances, the commands in the submenus have already been discussed in the section on the toolbar buttons.

*Using the
file menu
option*

As shown in Figure 3-6, the File submenu has 12 commands, the most of any submenu. The **File | Open Location…** and **File | Print…** submenu options are the same as the toolbar Open and Print buttons. (By **File | Open Location…** we mean Select File from the menu bar and then select **Open Location…** from the File submenu.) In this section, we will discuss the remaining File submenu options which are divided into four groups: Window and Mail commands, File commands, Printing commands, and Close or Exit commands.

Window and
mail commands

To open additional Netscape windows, you would use **File | New Window**. Recall that Windows allows multiple tasks to be undertaken at the same time and this includes having multiple Netscape windows open. For example, you can have Alberto's home page open in one window and the Margaritaville home page open in another window. You can resize or move the windows as needed or close a window with the Close command. Figure 3-7 shows two Netscape windows open simultaneously.

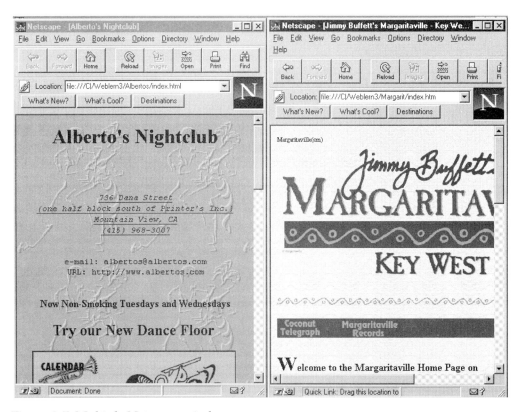

Figure 3-7. Multiple Netscape windows

As we have already mentioned, you can use the Netscape browser for e-mail and there are two options in the File menu associated with e-mail: New Mail Message and Mail Document. The first of these allows you to create and send a message while the second allows you to send a message plus the URL of the current document. We will discuss both options in more detail in Chapter 5 where we assume you have access to the Internet.

File commands: If you are accessing a Web page on the Internet, you can enter the URL by using the toolbar Open button or **File I Open Location...** . On the other hand, if you are accessing a local Web page, then you can enter a URL with the file:/// protocol or you can use the **File I Open File...** command. If the latter approach is used, the File Open dialog box is displayed as shown in Figure 3-8.

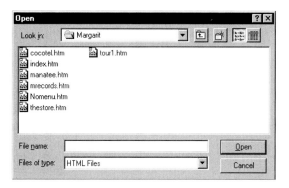

Figure 3-8. Open file dialog box

From the Open File dialog box, you can use the list boxes to select a drive (a:, c:, and so on), select a directory, and, then, select an htm file. For example, with Windows, you should look for the Weblern2 directory if it does not automatically appear. In the Weblern2 directory, you will see the htm file list for this directory plus a list of directories corresponding to the five Web sites discussed in Chapter 1.You can click on one of these directories to see the htm files in it and then click on an htm file and click OK to retrieve it. Note that since you are not required to go through a home page to view an associated Web page, *all* Web pages with an extension of htm are displayed in this list.

To save a Web page to disk with an htm extension (or html in Windows 95 or the Macintosh), you can use **File I Save As...** . If you select this command, then the **Save As...** dialog box displays a drive, directory, and file name. You can change any of these as needed. As discussed in Chapter 2, the images are *not* saved as a part of the local file that you are creating. If you retrieve a saved file into Netscape, it will look similar to the left side of Figure 3-4.

Earlier, we identified browsers as the *Swiss Army knife* of the Internet. The next File submenu option—**Upload Files...**—is a good example of the many capabilities of Netscape. If you are using Netscape to connect to an FTP site to which you have the rights to send files, then **File I Upload Files** will enable you to send file to the FTP site. This option is active only if the current page accesses an FTP site.

Printing com-
mands

By selecting **File | Page Setup...**, you can control the printing characteristics for the Web page in terms of the margins and the contents of the header and footer. To preview the Web page that will be printed if the Print button is clicked or the Print command selected, select **File | Print Preview**.

Close and exit
commands

Finally, to close a Netscape Window, select **File | Close**. Note: if you only have one Netscape window open, then selecting **File | Close** will have the same effect as **File | Exit**, that is, exiting Netscape.

- - - - - - - - - - - - - - - - - - - - - - - - -

## Your turn!

1. If the textbook home page is not displayed in Netscape, click on the Home button to display it. With a formatted disk in the a: drive, use the **File | Save As...** command to save the current Web page to your disk, with a name of a:\textbook.htm.

2. Use **File | New Window** to open a new Netscape window. Note that the textbook home page is displayed in this new window. Why? Now use **File | Open File...** to retrieve the a:\textbook.htm file into this window in Netscape. Resize this window and compare the two versions of the textbook home page. Use **File | Close** to close this window.

3. Use **File | Page Setup** to view the current information for the textbook home page. Now use **File | Print Preview** to see how the page would look if it were printed.

- - - - - - - - - - - - - - - - - - - - - - - - -

*Using the
edit sub-
menu*

The second menu option, Edit, may be one of the least used of the Netscape menu options. Of the first five commands, only two—Copy and Select All— can be used in the Netscape content area. The remaining commands, Undo, Cut, and Paste, are greyed out except when you have highlighted an *editable field* like the Location Window. The **Edit | Copy** command can be used to copy highlighted text in the content field to the Windows clipboard, where it can then be pasted into another Windows application, but not into the Netscape content screen. For example, the Copy command can be used to copy information from the Netscape screen into the e-mail window. The **Edit | Select All** command highlights all fields in the content field which can then be copied using the **Edit | Copy** command. If you highlight the contents of the Location Window, then the other three commands can be used.

The last two commands are the **Edit | Find** and **Edit | Find Again** commands which work just like the Find button on the toolbar.

## Using the view submenu

The View submenu has six options: Reload, Reload Frame, Load Images, Refresh, Document Source and Document Info. For our purposes, the **View | Reload** and **View | Refresh** commands are the same as the Reload button on the toolbar menu, and the **View | Load Images** command is the same as the Images button. The **View | Reload Frames** command will be discussed later. The last two commands, Document Source and Document Info, display information about the Web page. The **View | Document Source** command displays the HTML source code for the Web document. You can only view the source code; it cannot be created or modified with Netscape. The **View | Document Info** command displays information about the Web page, including the document title, URL, file type, page location, date of last modification, and other information about the security status of the Web page, and so on. Figure 2-9 showed the result of using the **View | Document Source** command for the UGA swim team home page. This menu also has the option to view the source document and document information for a Netscape feature known as frames in which the Netscape screen is divided into sections. Frames are discussed in more detail later in the chapter.

## Using the go submenu

The Go submenu has four commands, all of which are the same as toolbar buttons. The Back, Forward, and Home commands are the same as the toolbar buttons with the same names, while the Stop Loading command is the same as the Stop button. Below these commands is the **history list** which includes a partial list of recently visited Web sites with the current site having a checkmark beside it. You can go directly to a site in the history list by clicking on the Web page name. You can also select the View History command to see a more complete description of these pages. You should be aware that the history list only shows a partial list of Web pages, including the most recently visited Web page and any Web pages that can be reached from it. For example, assume you are at Page A and then go to Page B via a hypertext link. Now assume you go to Page C, and finally go to Page D, all via hypertext links. If you then use the history list to return to Page B and now use another hypertext link to go to, say, Page R, you will see that Pages C and D are no longer a part of the History List.

■ ■ ■ ■ ■ ■ ■ ■ ■ ■ ■ ■ ■ ■ ■ ■ ■ ■ ■ ■ ■ ■ ■

## Your turn!

1. Use the **Edit | Find** command to search for all occurrences of Richard Watson's name in the textbook home page.
2. Use the **View | Document Source** command to view the text document for the textbook home page.

3.  From the textbook home page, go to the ScubaNet home page and then to the Diveflag Swimsuit Web page. Click the Back button twice to return to the textbook home page and view the history list. Now select the ScubaNet home page and then return to the textbook page and view history again. How has it changed?

*Using the bookmarks submenu*

Recall from Chapter 2 that we discussed saving the URLs of interesting Web pages. To save the URL of the current home page or to access the URL of previously visited home pages in Netscape, use the Bookmark option. It has only two commands: Add Bookmark and Go to Bookmarks, plus a list of previously saved home pages and folders of saved pages. You may visit any of these home pages by simply clicking on its name. Or, you can see the bookmarks in a folder by positioning the highlighting over the folder name and then selecting a bookmark from within the folder by clicking on it.

You may add the current Web page to the Bookmark list by clicking on **Bookmarks | Add Bookmark**. If this is done and you click on Bookmarks again, you will note that it has been added. You may also view a more complete bookmark list by selecting **Bookmarks | Go to Bookmarks**. This action will display the Bookmark Window with a menu bar from which you can access File, Edit and Item options. These options enable you to find a particular bookmark, insert folders, or edit a bookmark. It also contains many features that are beyond the scope of this text. Figure 3-9 shows the Bookmark window resulting from the **Bookmarks | Go to Bookmarks** command.

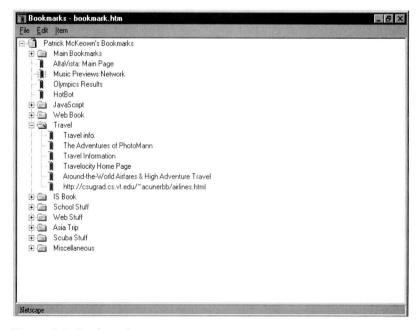

Figure 3-9. Bookmark screen

## Using the options submenu

The Options submenu has two primary purposes: to control the screen appearance and to set default settings for Netscape. We will only consider the first since changing default settings is beyond the scope of this text (and should NOT be done in a classroom environment by anyone other than the local network supervisor).

To control the screen appearance, simply select the Options submenu from the menu bar and note that there is the Preferences section with four types of preferences, which is used for default settings. This section is followed by five screen control selections. If an option has a checkmark beside it, then the item will be displayed. You can choose to display or not display the Toolbar, Location Window, or the Directory buttons by clicking on the first three options. The fourth Option, Show Java Console, is used when a computer language associated with Netscape called Java is running. You should not worry about this option. You can also control whether images are automatically loaded with a Web page with the fifth option. The last item in the Options submenu, Document Encoding, is beyond the scope of this text and should be ignored.

Since any options you change are automatically saved, you must be careful to always return any options that you change to their original status.

### Your turn!

1. Select the Bookmarks submenu and note the Web sites that are listed there. If the current page is not on the bookmark list, add it by selecting **Bookmarks | Add Bookmark**.

2. Select **Bookmarks | View** Bookmarks and select **Bookmarks | Go to Bookmarks**. Highlight one of the items in the Bookmark list and then select **File | Properties** to view information on this Bookmark item.

3. Select the Options submenu and note which items are checked. If the **Options | Show Directory Buttons** selection is checked, click on it. What happens to the screen's appearance? Now click on this selection again to return the screen to its original appearance. Do the same for the **Options | Toolbar** and **Options | Location** selections.

4. If **Options | Auto Load Images** is checked, click on it to erase the check. Now use the Open button to retrieve the Web page with URL file:///c:/weblern2/albertos/index.htm. Note that no images are displayed. Now use the Images button to display the images. Finally, click on **Options | Auto Load Images** to return it to its original state.

## Directory and help submenus

The sixth and eighth options on the menu bar are the Directory and Help submenus. These two options are different from all other menu options in that the submenus do not have commands; rather, they provide access to a wide variety of useful and interesting Web pages. These Web pages must be loaded from the Internet rather from a local disk, however. In addition, many of the submenu commands are also available from the Directory buttons, which we discuss in the next section. For these two reasons, we will not consider the Directory and Help menu options here. They will be discussed in Chapter 5, where you will be asked to visit Web sites on the Internet.

*Window option*

The next to last option on the menu bar is the Window option. This option provides access to the Netscape e-mail and Newsgroup clients. It can also be used to access and edit an e-mail address book which allows you to store e-mail addresses for those persons with whom you correspond frequently. The Window option also provides you with access to the Bookmark screen and an enhanced history screen that allows you to create bookmarks or go to the various sites. We will discuss the e-mail and newsgroup clients in Chapter 5.

**Directory buttons**

The bottom set of buttons in Netscape are referred to as the Directory buttons. These link to a variety of home pages that the developers of Netscape have made available to its users. All of these buttons require you to be able to access the Internet, so you should NOT click on any of them unless your instructor tells you to do so. As we stated earlier, these buttons differ between the various versions of Netscape. Figure 3-10 shows the Directory buttons for the Netscape Navigator 3.0. Because they depend on access to the Internet, the Directory buttons will be covered in more detail in Chapter 5. The last of the browser operations mentioned above: searching for Web pages of interest, will also be covered in that chapter.

Figure 3-10. Directory buttons

**Advanced topics: frames and popup menus**

Among the numerous new features offered by Netscape Navigator 2.x and 3.x over previous versions are frames and popup menus. **Frames** are a way to divide the monitor screen into sections or *panes* with each section containing a different Web page. These multiple Web pages are often designed to work together to provide more information than is possible with a single Web page. For example, if we retrieve the frames version of the UGA swim team Web page by clicking on this link from the textbook home page or by using the URL

file:///c:/weblern2/ugaswim/home.htm

the result is shown in Figure 3-11.

In Figure 3-11, you can see that the screen is divided into top and bottom sections. The top section or frame acts as a table of contents to the remainder of the Web site. For example, if you click on any of the links in the upper frame, you can immediately retrieve other pages in this Web site into the frame on the bottom, replacing the initial Web page which is the same one shown in Chapter 2. For example, by clicking on a link in the top frame, you can see information on the coaches, the team members, the new UGA Ramsey

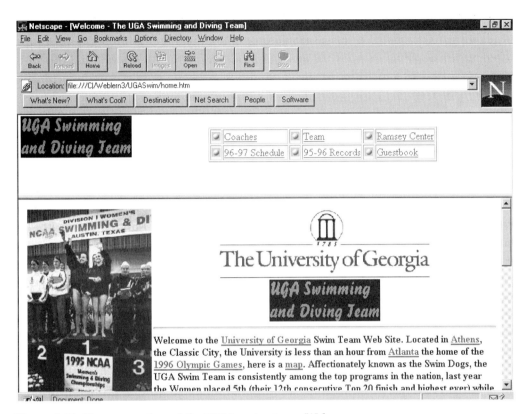

Figure 3-11. Frame version of the UGA swim team Web page

Center swimming facility, the 1996-97 schedule, or the 1995-96 records in the bottom frame. You can also *sign* a guest book indicating that you have visited this Web site. Figure 3-12 shows the change in the lower frame that results from clicking on the Ramsey Center link in the upper frame. Notice that it is possible to scroll up and down in the lower frame without changing the upper frame; frames operate independently of one another.

In addition to acting as a table of contents to the Web site, one frame can be used to control a document in another frame. For example, clicking on links in the control frame can take you to another part of the same document, to another document, or out of the document altogether. Frames can also be used as a **banner** that remains static while the lower frame changes. This is especially useful for displaying a corporate logo or copyright message on the screen at all times. It is also possible to display a form in one frame and to display the results of entering information in the form in another frame.

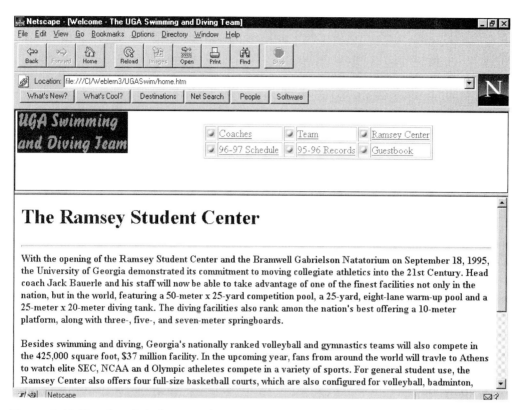

Figure 3-12. Results of clicking on the link in the upper frame

*Navigating in frames with popup menus*

Obviously, frames dramatically increase the amount of information that can be displayed on the screen. However, they can be confusing to navigate. To help you understand navigating in frames, you first need to understand that only one frame at a time can have the *focus*, that is, be the active frame. To change a different active frame, you simply click anywhere inside it. When you select a frame, you will notice that the border of the frame changes. You can also change the size of the selected frame by locating the cursor on the separator between it and other frames and dragging the separator (the cursor changes shape).

When you are working with frames and you change the contents of a frame by clicking on a hypertext link, then the Back and Forward toolbar buttons do not pertain to the selected frame. To move backward and forward in frames, you need to use **popup menus**. This type menu is displayed in the content area by clicking on the *right* mouse button in Windows (or holding down the mouse button on the Macintosh). Figure 3-13 shows a popup menu in the bottom frame of the UGA swim team Web page with frame navigation options. Note that *Back in frame* is active; if you click on this option, you will go back to the previous contents of the same frame. If the Web page does not have any frames, the popup menu has options that replicate the actions of the back and forward toolbar buttons. There is also an option to add a bookmark to the Web page in this frame. Since we are working in Windows 95, there is also an option that enables you to create a shortcut to this Web page from the desktop.

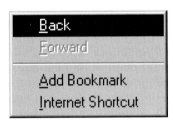

Figure 3-13. Popup menu for frame navigation

If you right-click on a Web page with a **background image**, that is a transparent image which is repeated over all the Web page, you are also given the option to save this background image to disk or to set it as your Windows wallpaper. Finally, If you activate the popup menu with the mouse pointer over an image, it has additional options that enable you to carry out a variety of actions with the image including viewing it by itself, saving it to disk, copying its URL to the Windows clipboard, and, if the image is not currently displayed, displaying it on the screen. The image version of the popup menu is shown in Figure 3-14.

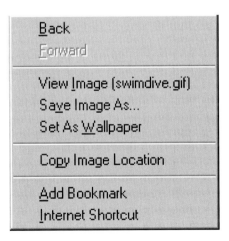

Figure 3-14. Popup menu for images

*Other frame options*

In addition to the popup menu frame options, some Menu bar options change when a Web page containing frames is retrieved. These frame-related options exist in the File and View Menu bar options. In the File submenu, there are three differences between Web pages with and without frames. For pages with frames, the **File | Mail Document** option becomes **File | Mail Frame**, the

69

**File | Save As...** option becomes **File | Save Frame As...**, and the **File | Print...** option becomes **File | Print Frame...** In each case, the File submenu option pertains to the active frame rather than to the entire Web page. In the View submenu, the Reload Frame option which is greyed out for nonframes pages is now available for reloading the contents of the active frame.

## Your turn!

1. Retrieve the frames version of the UGA swim team Web page by clicking on the appropriate link in the textbook home page or by using the URL
   file:///c:/weblern2/ugaswim/home.htm
   Now click in the top frame to change the focus and then click on the Ramsey Center link to see a Web page like that shown in Figure 3-12.

2. Use the popup menu in the Ramsey Center Web page and click on Back in Frames to return to the original Web page.

3. Use the popup menu in the UGA swim team Web page to go forward to the Ramsey Center page. Go to the Table of Contents page in the top frame and click on the Coaches link to retrieve the corresponding Web page.

4. Use the popup menu with the mouse pointer over the picture of the coaches and then click on View this Image to see the image by itself. Click the Toolbar back button to return to the Coaches frame.

5. For the Coaches frame, use the **File | Save Frame As...** option to save this frame to your disk in the a: drive as coaches.htm.

## Key terms and concepts

| | |
|---|---|
| background image | mouse pointer |
| banner | opening home page |
| disk cache | point and click navigation |
| frames | popup menu |
| history list | progress bar |
| mail indicator | security area |
| memory cache | shortcut key |
| menu bar | toolbar |

## Exercises

1. List and describe the parts of the Netscape screen discussed in the text. List and briefly discuss three of the ways to access a Web page.

2.  What are the three types of buttons on the toolbar. Which button can be used to stop the retrieval of a Web page? Why would this be necessary for a remote Web page but not for a local Web page?

3.  What are the four steps that a browser goes through to retrieve a remote Web page? What are the two types of cache that are available with Netscape? Which is permanent?

4.  What is a shortcut key in Netscape? What are the three ways to select an option from the menu bar?

5.  What are the three ways to make a selection from a drop down submenu in Netscape?

6.  How does the Open File selection from the File submenu differ from the Open Location selection or the Open toolbar button? Can you obtain the same results from the Open Location selection as you do from the Open File selection?

7.  What are the Directory buttons used for? Why don't we discuss their use with local Web pages?

For the following seven exercises, you should be working at a computer.

8.  Access Netscape. If you do not find the textbook home page shown in Figure 3-1, press the Home Toolbar button. If this does not display the textbook home page, press the Open Toolbar button and enter the URL (assuming you are accessing the local files from a hard disk): file:///c:/weblern2/webbook.htm

9.  From the textbook home page, click on the hypertext link to Jimmy Buffett's Margaritaville home page. Open a new Web page and tile the two windows. Close the second window.

10. Use the Open File option to retrieve the ScubaNet local Web page which is found at c:\weblern2\scubanet\index.htm and then check the history list in two ways. Also, check the bookmark list in two ways. Look at the text version of the document and then return to the ScubaNet page.

11. Go back to the textbook home page and turn off autoloading of images. Click on the Rhebok link to open the local Rhebok Winery home page and note the form in which the page is loaded. Use the popup menu to view the image. When was the Rhebok Winery founded? Turn image loading back on and reload the page.

12. Scroll down to the bottom of the Rhebok Winery home page. Select the Restaurant Web page from the list of Rhebok pages and go to it. Click on the photo of the restaurant to enlarge it. Use the popup menu to view the image on a separate page. Return to the Rhebok home page.

13. Turn off display of the Toolbar and the Directory buttons. Also, turn off display of the Location Window. What happens to the screen? Can you turn off display of the Menu bar? Now turn display of the Toolbar and Directory buttons and Location Window back on. Save this page to your floppy disk with a name of rhebok.htm.

14. Go back to the textbook home page and select the home page for Alberto's Nightclub. Use the Find toolbar button to search for occurrences of the word *calendar*. How many such occurrences are there on this home page. Scroll down this page and view the image shown there. Use the File Print Preview command to view the form of this page if it were printed.

■ ▬ ▬ ▬ ▬ ▬ ▬ ▬ ▬ ▬ ▬ ▬ ▬ ▬ ▬ ▬ ▬ ▬ ▬ ▬ ▬ ▬ ▬ ■

# 4      Creating Web documents

**Objectives**

After completing this chapter, you will be able to:

❖ describe the key features of HTML;

❖ define the difference between logical and physical styles;

❖ define the difference between absolute and relative addressing;

❖ create a Web application using HTML;

❖ understand form and map processing.

**What is HTML?**

You learned in Chapter 1 that the Web is a client/server system in which the client is called a **browser**. The **server** contains text files that are converted by the browser for display on a monitor. To do this, the browser needs instructions for preparing a text file, instructions that are written in the **Hypertext Markup Language (HTML)**. The basic component of the language is a **tag**, which tells the browser how to display data. For example, the following HTML statement

```
<cite>Computerworld</cite> is a weekly newspaper
for information systems professionals.
```

is displayed as

*Computerworld* is a weekly newspaper for information systems professionals.

The tags **<cite>** and **</cite>** around *Computerworld* inform the browser that this word (i.e., *Computerworld*) must be displayed in citation format (italics in this case). Tags often travel in pairs, encircling the text to be displayed in a particular style. They are almost identical, except for the trailing tag, which has a distinguishing slash (/). As this small example illustrates, HTML is a simple language for describing how a text file will be displayed by a browser, thus explaining the presence of Markup[1] in HTML.

Failure to use the terminating tag of a pair will mean that the option remains turned on, and thus the option applies to all following text in the document. As you will soon discover, some tags (e.g., **<p>**, **<br>**, and **<hr>**) do not require a terminating tag.

What does the hypertext part of HTML mean? Ordinary text, like this book, is linear; sentences are arranged sequentially, and the author expects that you will read large portions of the text sequentially. Sometimes, as discussed in Chapters 1 and 2, you may want to refer to other parts of the book. Imagine you are reading a sentence containing the acronym HTML, and you don't know what it means. Typically, you would turn to the book's glossary for a definition. Now, imagine you are reading the Web version of this book. When you come across HTML (assuming it is a defined hypertext link), you simply click on the acronym, and the browser retrieves the page containing its definition. After reading the definition, you click on the return icon, a left-pointing arrow, to return to the point where you clicked on HTML. A text that supports electronic linking to other parts of the document or other documents is called **hypertext**. When creating a hypertext document, the author needs to decide which items in a text should be linked to other items, create the link, and then indicate to the reader that a link exists. Creating and denoting a link is easy. The hard part is identifying all the words or phrases that should be linked.

As you are aware from using a browser, a Web document can include **multimedia** objects—images, video, and audio. HTML also includes instructions for defining what type of object to include and where it is stored on the server. There are also features of HTML for handling forms and electronic mail. Because it is possible to define an image as a **hyperlink** (i.e., clicking on the image links you to another page), the term **hypermedia** is often associated with the HTML.

In summary, HTML is a language for:

1. describing how a Web browser should display a text file retrieved from a server;
2. describing hyperlinks;
3. defining multimedia objects included with a Web document.

You can create a HTML file using any editor or word processor. We will assume that you have access to and are familiar with the editor supplied with your computer's operating system (e.g., Notepad for Windows 3.1, Wordpad for Windows 95, or SimpleText for Macintosh). Remember to save HTML files as text files.

---

1. Markup is a publishing industry term for describing the size, style, and position of each typographical element on a page.

## The form of a HTML document

A HTML document has some standard tags to define its major components. The **<html>** and **</html>** tags indicate the beginning and end of a HTML document. The next pair of tags **<head>** and **</head>**, define the document's head which contains the title—indicated by the **<title>** and **</title>** tags. The title is displayed in the title bar. Finally, the body of the document lies within the **<body>** and **</body>** tags. It is good practice to first define these tags before writing any other parts of the HTML document. HTML commands to create a simple Web page are shown in Figure 4-1. The resulting Web browser display is illustrated in Figure 4-2. Observe that the title of the document (Web document #1) appears in the title bar.

```
<html>
<head>
<title>Web document #1</title>
</head>
<body>
The body of document #1
</body>
</html>
```

Figure 4-1. HTML to describe a simple Web page

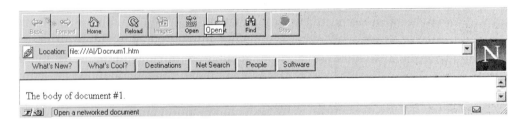

Figure 4-2. A simple Web page

*Head*

The main feature of the head element is the title. Each document should have a meaningful title of less than 64 characters. The title, displayed in the title section of the browser's window, should identify a document's content. A meaningful title helps visitors identify the contents of a page.

*Body*

The content of a HTML document is contained with the body, which contains the text and images seen by someone browsing the page. HTML elements (e.g., heading, list, hypertext link) define the elements of a document.

## Your turn!

1. Double click on your editor's icon. Enter the contents of Figure 4-1.
2. Select File Save As... and enter a document name as a:\docnum1.htm. Select the file Type as *.Txt (text file) and click on OK.
3. Minimize your editor and then access Netscape. Click on the Open button and enter the URL as file:///a:\docnum1.htm. The result should look like Figure 4-2.

*Headings*

Nearly every document uses headings to indicate new sections and subsections. The six heading levels of HTML are labeled h1, h2, ..., h6. As a general rule, use h1 for the main heading, h2 for the next level heading, and so forth for less important headings. The interpretation of heading levels varies by browser, but the presentation in Table 4-1 gives an indication of what you can expect.

Table 4-1: Heading levels

| Heading level | Server | Browser |
|---|---|---|
| 1 | `<h1>Heading h1</h1>` | Heading h1 |
| 2 | `<h2>Heading h2</h2>` | Heading h2 |
| 3 | `<h3>Heading h3</h3>` | Heading h3 |
| 4 | `<h4>Heading h4</h4>` | Heading h4 |
| 5 | `<h5>Heading h5</h5>` | Heading h5 |
| 6 | `<h6>Heading h6</h6>` | Heading h6 |

Note: The standard format for illustrating HTML features is to show the HTML commands as stored on the server and the resulting browser displays side-by-side under two columns headed *Server* and *Browser*, respectively.

*Paragraph*

The paragraph element, **<p>**, indicates a paragraph break. Use it to separate blocks of text, just as you do in standard writing. A paragraph break is not required for headings or list elements.

*Line break*

The line break element, **<br>**, indicates the start of a new line. It is like a hard *carriage return*. In comparison, the **<p>** element defines a block of text. Use it to break lines in a limerick (see Table 4-2).

Table 4-2: A break **<br>** example

| Server | Browser |
|---|---|
| There was a young lady named Bright<br><br>Who traveled much faster than light.<br><br>She started one day<br><br>In a relative way<br><br>And came back on the previous night.<br> | There was a young lady named Bright<br>Who traveled much faster than light.<br>She started one day<br>In a relative way<br>And came back on the previous night. |

## Horizontal rule

The horizontal rule, **<hr>**, is used to draw a horizontal line across a screen. It is a stronger form of text separation than a paragraph break. It can be used at the bottom of a page to separate the details about the owner from the preceding text (see Table 4-3).

Table 4-3: A horizontal rule **<hr>** example

| Server | Browser |
|---|---|
| <hr><br>This page is maintained by Fred Bloggs (fredb@meekatharra.au), who is responsible for all errors and omissions. | ————————————<br>This page is maintained by Fred Bloggs (fredb@meekatharra.au), who is responsible for all errors and omissions. |

## Comments

**Comments** can be embedded in a HTML document to help the person who wrote the code or is maintaining it understand its purpose. Comments are indicated by the special character strings **<!--** and **-->**. The string (**<!--**) is the start of a comment and (**-->**) is its end. Anything between these strings is a comment and is not displayed by the browser (see Table 4-4). Comments are for humans to process, not browsers. As some browsers mishandle comments that run across more than one line, it is a good idea to include comment strings on every line you wish to annotate.

Table 4-4: A comment example

| Server | Browser |
|---|---|
| <!-- A comment      --> | |

■ ■ ■ ■ ■ ■ ■ ■ ■ ■ ■ ■ ■ ■ ■ ■ ■ ■ ■ ■

## Your turn!

1. Minimize Netscape, maximize your editor. Open a:\docnum1.htm.

2. Erase the line in this document: "The body of document #1."

3. Use the H1 heading type to create a new first line of text, "My home page."

4. Use the H2 heading type to create a second line of text "by" followed by your name. For example, the second line of text might read, "by Ned Watson."

5. Use the <hr> tag to create a horizontal line beneath your name.

6. Type your local address (including your e-mail address, if you have one) on the next two or three lines and end each line with the line break <br> tag.

7. Save the new version of a:\docnum1.htm. Minimize your editor, maximize Netscape, and use the Reload button to bring in the revised version of the Web page.

■ ■ ■ ■ ■ ■ ■ ■ ■ ■ ■ ■ ■ ■ ■ ■ ■ ■ ■ ■

## HTML style tags

**Style tags** define how text will appear when displayed by a browser. There are two types of styles applied to groups of characters, words, or sentences: physical and logical. Bold, italics, and underlining are examples of **physical styles**. Emphasis, strong emphasis, and cite are instances of **logical styles**.

Logical and physical styles are used for segments of text within a paragraph. If you wish to apply a logical style to a block of text, you have three choices: preformatted, block quote, and address. For instance, you would use the block quote style to surround a piece of text that is a quote rather than using emphasis. As a result, it is then possible with appropriate software to identify all the quotes in a document by searching for blockquote tags.

## Physical styles

Physical styles are illustrated in Table 4-5. The only style that may need additional explanation is <tt> (typewriter), which specifies a monospaced typewriter font, such as Courier. Physical styles should be avoided because some browsers may not handle them.

Table 4-5: Physical styles

| Style | Server | Browser |
|---|---|---|
| Bold | `<b>Text style</b>` | **Text style** |
| Italics | `<i>Text style</i>` | *Text style* |
| Underline | `<u>Text style</u>` | <u>Text style</u> |
| Typewriter | `<tt>Text style</tt>` | Text style |

## Logical styles

The usual rendering of logical styles, the preferred form for styles, is shown in Table 4-6. For example, italics are used for emphasis (em). The interpretation of logical styles may not be distinct—emphasis and cite usually display as italics. Some browsers permit customization of logical styles, so you could specify that stronger (strong) will display in purple type.

Table 4-6: Logical styles

| Style | Tag | Usual rendering | Server | Browser |
|---|---|---|---|---|
| Emphasis | em | Italics | `<em>Text style</em>` | *Text style* |
| Stronger emphasis | strong | Bold | `<strong>Text style</strong>` | **Text style** |
| Citation | cite | Italics | `<cite>Text style</cite>` | *Text style* |
| Computer code | code | Monospaced | `<code>Text style</code>` | Text style |

Preformatted

A block of text, such as computer code, can be displayed in a monospaced font using the **<pre>** and **</pre>** tags (see Table 4-7).

Table 4-7: A preformatted text **<pre>** example

| Server | Browser |
|---|---|
| `<pre>`<br>`sum = 0`<br>`for indx = 1 to 50`<br>`    sum = sum + obs(indx)`<br>`next indx`<br>`</pre>` | `sum = 0`<br>`for indx = 1 to 50`<br>`    sum = sum + obs(indx)`<br>`next indx` |

Block quote

Quoted text is defined using the **<blockquote>** and **</blockquote>** tags. A browser may indent or italicize the text. A block quote forces a paragraph break and a blank line before and after the quoted text (see Table 4-8).

Table 4-8: A block quote **<blockquote>** example

| Server | Browser |
|---|---|
| `Groucho Marx:<blockquote>What's a thousand dollars? Mere chicken feed. A poultry matter.`<br>`</blockquote>`<br>`In the film, <em>Cocoanuts.</em>` | Groucho Marx:<br>    What's a thousand dollars? Mere chicken feed. A poultry matter.<br>In the film, *Cocoanuts.* |

---

**A very personal experience**

We wrote the first edition of this book using different word processors (WordPerfect and Microsoft Word) on different platforms (Windows and Macintosh). We exchanged files using FTP. A final camera ready version was created using FrameMaker on a Macintosh PowerPC. The final version was printed on a 600 dpi printer and mailed to the publisher.

The process was not completely seamless. For example, WordPerfect on Windows could not successfully translate Microsoft Word for the Mac files. Thus, we had to convert Macintosh Word files first to Windows Word files and then to Word Perfect format.

Why didn't we standardize on the same word processor and operating system? Because one of us is a Mac fanatic and the other a recalcitrant Windows Word Perfect user.

Why did we change to FrameMaker instead of using Word or WordPerfect for the camera ready reversion? Because we found we needed the full functionality of document publishing software to manage the placement of tables and figures.

We made several changes for the second edition. We stayed with our preferred operating system, but changed word processors to Word (Windows) and FrameMaker (Mac). Why the change? We found that the conversion of Word to FrameMaker was more efficient than using WordPerfect, and it was also more efficient to write directly in FrameMaker rather than preparing text using a word processor and converting.

Another change was to create a computer ready version of the text, which was electronically transmitted using FTP (see "FTP" on page 116) to the publisher. Reviewers of the book, who made many helpful suggestions for improving this edition, were able to retrieve the chapters electronically, as PDF files (see "Electronic documents" on page 120), from a private Web site. These changes enabled us to reduce the time needed to create a second version by several weeks and thus deliver a more timely text.

---

Address

The address mode is normally used for addresses, signatures, and details about the author (see Table 4-9). You will often find this information at the end of a document. Note the use of <br> to indicate a line break at the end of each line of the address.

Table 4-9: An address **<address>** example

| Server | Browser |
|--------|---------|
| `<address>`<br>`Richard T. Watson<br>`<br>`Department of Management<br>`<br>`University of Georgia<br>`<br>`Athens, GA 30602-6256<br>`<br>`</address>` | *Richard T. Watson*<br>*Department of Management*<br>*University of Georgia*<br>*Athens, GA 30602-6256* |

## Your turn!

1. Minimize Netscape, maximize your editor, and, if it is not already opened, open the file a:\docnum1.htm.

2. Add a new horizontal line beneath your address.

3. Add a new line to the file starting with the word "Major:" strongly emphasized, followed by your major emphasized. Add a line break tag after this line.

4. Add the Address tag to the two or three lines of your address that you entered earlier.

5. Save the new version of a:\docnum1.htm. Minimize your editor, maximize Netscape, and use the Reload button to bring in the revised version of the Web page.

## Lists

Three types of **lists** can be defined: regular, menu, and descriptive. A regular list is a sequence of paragraphs, a menu list is an interactive menu of choices, and a descriptive list is an inventory of items where each is followed by a descriptive paragraph.

## Regular list

A regular list is used for displaying a list of items, which may be bulleted (**<ul>**) (also known as unordered) or numbered (**<ol>**) (also known as ordered). A list is surrounded by a pair of tags, and each list element is preceded by a **<li>** tag (see Table 4-10).

Table 4-10: List examples

| Type of list | Server | Browser |
|---|---|---|
| UL<br>(unordered) | \<ul><br>\<li> Seoul<br>\<li> Barcelona<br>\<li> Atlanta<br>\</ul> | • Seoul<br>• Barcelona<br>• Atlanta |
| OL<br>(ordered) | \<ol><br>\<li> Washington<br>\<li> Adams<br>\<li> Jefferson<br>\</ol> | 1. Washington<br>2. Adams<br>3. Jefferson |

*Menu list*     A menu list is recommended for situations in which a choice is made from several links. The result is similar to an unordered list (see Table 4-10). Don't be concerned if you don't understand all of the HTML commands used in Table 4-11; they will be covered shortly. The main things to notice are the **\<menu>** and**\<li>** tags.

Table 4-11: A menu list example

| Server | Browser |
|---|---|
| ```<h2>Useful information for visitors to Paris</h2>```<br>```<menu>```<br>```<li> <a href="glossary.html"> Paris glossary</a>```<br>```<li> <a href="telephone.html"> Telephone</a>```<br>```</menu>``` | **Useful information for visitors to Paris**<br><br>• Paris glossary<br>• Telephone |

*Descriptive list*     A glossary, a good application of a descriptive list, comprises a term and its definition. The boundaries of a descriptive list are defined by **\<dl>** and **\</dl>** tags. The example (see Table 4-12) illustrates that **\<dt>** precedes the name of the term and **\<dd>** precedes the definition of the term.

Table 4-12: A descriptive list example

| Server | Browser |
|---|---|
| ```html<br><H3>Paris trains</H3><br><dl><br><dt><strong>M&eacute;tro<br></strong><br><dd>The Paris subway. It is<br>extensive and serves nearly every<br>corner of the city. The last<br>trains are around 00h30.<br><dt><strong>RER</strong><br><dd>R&eacute;seau Express<br>R&eacute;gional; similar to the<br>M&eacute;tro except that it also<br>serves the outlying suburbs and<br>regions of Paris. In the center<br>of the city, the distance between<br>RER stations is more significant<br>than for the M&eacute;tro; an<br>advantage if you want to cover<br>larger distances quickly--even in<br>the center of the city.<br></dl><br>``` | ### Paris trains<br><br>**Métro**<br><br>The Paris subway. It is extensive and serves nearly every corner of the city. The last trains are around 00h30.<br><br>**RER**<br><br>Réseau Express Régional; similar to the Métro except that it also serves the outlying suburbs and regions of Paris. In the center of the city, the distance between RER stations is more significant than for the Métro; an advantage if you want to cover larger distances quickly--even in the center of the city. |

## Your turn!

1. Minimize Netscape, maximize your editor, and, if it is not already opened, open the file a:\docnum1.htm.

2. Beneath the line that displays your major, add a new line "Favorite Courses" that is underlined. End the line with a line break tag.

3. Add an ordered list of the three or four favorite courses that you have taken in your college career. (Naturally, you will want to include the current course!)

4. Add a new line "Other Courses" that is underlined with a line break.

5. Add an unordered list of three or four other courses that you have taken in your college career.

6. Save the new version of a:\docnum1.htm. Minimize your editor, maximize Netscape, and use the Reload button to bring in the revised version of the Web page.

## Anchors and images

The use of hyperlinks and hypermedia makes the Web easy to navigate and visually stimulating. These two features, easily implemented using HTML, are the focus of this section.

The **anchor tag** pair is the cornerstone of HTML's hypertext capabilities. It indicates the name of an object to be retrieved by the browser from a server. The object can be another Web document or some text within the current Web page. The anchor structure is also used to support e-mail. Mastering the use of anchors is critical to the creation of a link within and between Web pages. Every anchor has four components (see Figure 4-3). All anchors begin with "**<a**" and end with "**</a>**." An anchor specifies the address of the document or text to be retrieved, with the format varying with the type of anchor. Finally, an anchor usually has associated text to indicate the result of clicking on the link.

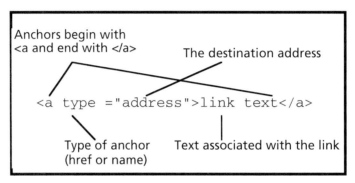

Figure 4-3. Components of an anchor

A major benefit of hypertext is that you can decompose a large linear document into smaller, logical chunks that can be reached using hyperlinks. There are two approaches to creating these logical chunks. First, you can keep the text as one physical file and create destination points within the text (linking within a document). Alternatively, you can make each logical chunk a separate file with a unique URL (linking to another document). Also, you can have a combination of these two approaches (linking to a destination within another document). These three approaches result in three different formats for anchors with a type of href (hypertext **ref**erence). A fourth href format is used for e-mail and can be thought of as linking to a person (see Table 4-13).

The other anchor type, name, is used to name a destination point within a document. It has to be a different type (name instead of href) so that a browser can distinguish between a destination within a document and a link to another document (see Table 4-14).

Table 4-13: The href type anchors

| Type | Format |
|------|--------|
| Linking within a document | `<a href="#identifier">link text</a>` |
| Linking to another document | `<a href="URL">link text</a>` |
| Linking to a destination within another document | `<a href="URL#identifier">link text</a>` |
| Sending e-mail | `<a href="mailto:e-mail address">link text</a>` |

Table 4-14: The name type anchor

| Type | Format |
|------|--------|
| Destination point within a document | `<a name="identifier">destination text</a>` |

## Linking within a document

Dividing a document into named destination points makes it possible to link to a place within the same document. Although any place within a document can be a destination point, it is generally a heading or subheading. Consider the case in which the document begins with a table of contents, a common use of links within a document (see Table 4-15). The name of each destination point is preceded by a #. In this case, *leftbank* is the name of the destination point.

Table 4-15: Linking within a document

| Server | Browser |
|--------|---------|
| `<menu>` <br> `<li><a href="#leftbank">Left Bank</a>` <br> ... <br> `</menu>` <br> ... <br> `<strong> <a name="leftbank">Left Bank (Rive Gauche)</a></strong>` | • <u>Left Bank</u> <br> ... <br><br><br><br> **Left Bank (Rive Gauche)** |

Every destination point must be uniquely labeled and accompanied by a corresponding HTML code to denote it. Within the document, the name[2] reference **<a name="leftbank">** denotes the destination point of a link. Thus if you click on <u>Left Bank</u> in the menu (the href anchor), the browser will jump to

---

2. More recent specifications of HTML are likely to use id rather than name, but this should not cause any problems.

the text beginning **Left Bank (Rive Gauche)**, the name anchor. You can have many href anchors linking to one name anchor, but every name anchor must be unique, or the browser will be confused.

*Linking to another document*

To create a link to another page, simply specify the URL. If the page is on another Web server, then the full URL must be given. Specifying the full URL is called absolute addressing. The first example in Table 4-16 illustrates use of **absolute addressing**.

Table 4-16: Linking to other documents

| Type of addressing | Server | Browser |
|---|---|---|
| Absolute | `<a href="http://www.uga.edu/">`<br>`University of Georgia</a>` | University of Georgia |
| Relative | `<a href="wineshop.htm">`<br>`Wine Shop</a>` | Wine Shop |
| Relative | `<a href="../Rhebok/winery.htm">`<br>`Rhebokskloof Estate</a>` | Rhebokskloof Estate |

If the file is on the same server, then only the path portion of the URL should be specified. This is called *relative addressing*. The second example in Table 4-16 demonstrates relative addressing where the desired document is in the same directory as the current document. The example describes a situation where the current document, index.htm, and the document it references, wineshop.htm, are both in the Rhebok directory (see Figure 4-4).

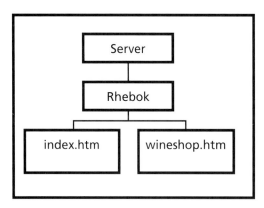

Figure 4-4. Relative addressing within the same directory

The third example in Table 4-16 illustrates **relative addressing** where the document to be retrieved is in another directory on the same server. The ".." indicates a path relative to the root directory for the server. The example describes a situation where the current document, index.htm, and the document it references, winery.htm, are in different directories (see Figure 4-5).

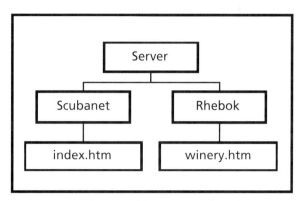

Figure 4-5. Relative addressing within the same server

Relative addressing should be used whenever possible because it makes HTML files transportable. If absolute addressing is used for every anchor, then moving a set of HTML files to another server can mean extensive editing (e.g., changing every occurrence of www.widget.com to www.thing.com in every HTML file); relative addressing will mean very few changes.

*Linking to a destination point within another document*

To link to specific points within another document, combine the principles of linking between and within documents. The following anchor illustrates a link from another server to www.cba.uga.edu and then to a particular point within a document:

```
<a href="http://www.cba.uga.edu/management/
phd.html#courses"> University of Georgia,
Ph. D. in Management courses</a>
```

The browser first finds the named server (www.cba.uga.edu), locates the desired document on that server (management/phd.html), searches for the anchor named courses within that document, and then displays the document starting at that location.

■ ■ ■ ■ ■ ■ ■ ■ ■ ■ ■ ■ ■ ■ ■ ■ ■ ■ ■ ■ ■ ■ ■ ■ ■

## Your turn!

1. Minimize Netscape, maximize your editor, and open the file a:\docnum1.htm.

2. Beneath the first horizontal line tag on this page, insert a level three heading "Parts of my page" and then use the menu tag to create a table of contents for your Web page.

3. Your menu should show two choices: Personal Information and School Information. The Personal Information choice should be linked to your address information, and the School Information choice should be linked to your major and course information.

4. Create a link to a document on the server set up to support this book. The URL of this document is http://www.negia.net/webbook, and it has useful information about the authors of this book.

5. Save the new version of a:\docnum1.htm. Minimize your editor, maximize Netscape, and use the Reload button to bring in the revised version of the Web page.

6. Click on each of the links you created to determine if your links are working correctly. Use the Back button to return to the original location in the Web page.

■ ■ ■ ■ ■ ■ ■ ■ ■ ■ ■ ■ ■ ■ ■ ■ ■ ■ ■ ■ ■ ■ ■ ■ ■ ■

*Linking to e-mail*

Most browsers (e.g., Netscape) incorporate an e-mail link. Imagine that you place your resumé on the Web, and you want to ensure that potential employers can contact you. In addition to giving your phone number, you may want to also state your e-mail address. Even better, set up an e-mail link so that commencing communication requires just a single click (see Table 4-17).

Table 4-17: An e-mail link

| Server | Browser |
|---|---|
| `For further information, e-mail <a href="mailto:president@whitehouse.gov"> The President</a>` | For further information, e-mail <br> <u>The President</u> |

When the e-mail link is selected, a message window appears (see Figure 5-7 on page 110). The browser inserts the sender's address information in the From field (this information must have been previously defined) and the receiver's e-mail address in the Mail to field. The sender then completes the rest of the message and clicks on the Send button.

*Loading an image*

**Images** make Web pages interesting. A corporate logo, a picture of a building, or a map can often explain far more than pages of text. Images are stored in a format that can be read by the browser. Files stored in the most popular formats, GIF and JPEG, are easily identified by the file extensions of gif and jpeg (jpg for Windows).

If you have an image file in gif or jpeg format, then it is very easy to write the HTML to display the image (see Figure 4-6). The image tag starts with the identifier, img scr=, to indicate an image is being defined. Next comes the URL of the file. The final component is the optional alignment specification--

text that is associated with the image but aligned with the bottom (the default), middle, or top of the image.

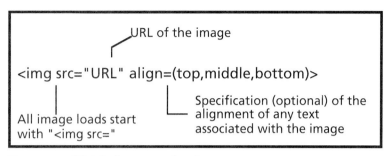

Figure 4-6. HTML for image loading

The example in Table 4-17 shows the effect of each of the alignment options. In the first case, there is no associated text. The other three examples illustrate the use of top, middle, and bottom alignment.

Table 4-18: Alignment options

| Browser | Server |
|---|---|
| `<img src=infoicon.gif>` | ![info icon] |
| `<h1><img src=infoicon.gif align=top> Paris Visitors' Center </h1>` | ![info icon] **Paris Visitors' Center** |
| `<h1><img src=infoicon.gif align=middle> Paris Visitors' Center </h1>` | ![info icon] **Paris Visitors' Center** |
| `<h1><img src=infoicon.gif align=bottom> Paris Visitors' Center </h1>` | ![info icon] **Paris Visitors' Center** |

*Setting the background color*

Standard gray is a bit boring for the background color of a Web page. Within the body tag, you can specify the background color by indicating its rgb code (red-green-blue). Every color can be created by combining appropriate proportions of red, green, and blue. The proportion of each color is specified as an 8-bit hexadecimal code (i.e., it can take values in the range 00 to ff). For example, to set the background to full red use **<body bgcolor = "#ff0000">** and to set it to white, use **<body bgcolor = "#ffffff">**.

*Setting the background image*

When you get tired of a plain color background, you can add some wallpaper. Any image can be used to tile a background, where an image is repeated like tiles on a floor or wall. Since text and other images are superimposed on the background image, it is a good idea to select a light-colored image. We tiled the background for this book's Web site by specifying **<body background="butterbk.gif">** where butterbk.gif is a very light blue butterfly.

■ ▬ ■ ▬ ■ ▬ ■ ▬ ■ ■ ▬ ■ ▬ ■ ■ ▬ ■ ▬ ■ ▬ ■ ▬ ■ ■

# Your turn!

1. Minimize Netscape, maximize your editor, and open the file a:\docnum1.htm. At the very beginning of your Web page, create an image link to the file metamorp.gif found in C:\weblrn2. Place the label "Metamorphosis" at the top of the image.

2. Save the new version of a:\docnum1.htm. Minimize your editor, maximize Netscape, and use the Reload button to bring in the revised version of the Web page. Note the placement of the image and label.

3. What color do you get with a background of full red and full green?

4. Create a background using metamorp.gif. Is it a suitable background?

■ ▬ ■ ▬ ■ ▬ ■ ▬ ■ ■ ▬ ■ ▬ ■ ■ ▬ ■ ▬ ■ ▬ ■ ▬ ■ ■

## Advanced features

The usefulness of a HTML document often can be enhanced by tables, forms, or maps. **Tables** make sets of data more readable; **forms** are the basis of many interactive applications (e.g., taking customers' orders); and **maps** are navigational aids. In addition, **special characters** improve the readability of documents because they permit the representation of characters such as é and ã.

*Tables*

The table markup commands support the presentation of tabular information. An example (see Figure 4-7) and resulting browser display (see Figure 4-8) demonstrate the use of table markup commands.

A table definition is enclosed by the tags **<table border>** and **</table>**. The **<caption>** and **</caption>** tags surround a table's caption. A column or row heading is preceded by a **<th>** tag. For instance, "**<th>** Month" indicates that Month is a heading cell (a column heading in this case because it follows the table's caption). The **<td>** tag precedes a cell's data (e.g., **<td>** March). The end of each row is signified by a **<tr>** tag.

```
<table border>
<Caption>Average daily maximum and minimum temperatures</cap-
tion>
<th> Month <th> Max (F) <th> Max (C) <th> Min (F) <th> Min (C) <tr>
<td> January <td> 43 <td> 6 <td> 34 <td> 1 <tr>
<td> February <td> 45 <td> 7 <td> 34 <td> 1 <tr>
<td> March <td> 54 <td> 12 <td> 39 <td> 4 <tr>
<td> April <td> 60 <td> 16 <td> 43 <td> 6 <tr>
<td> May <td> 68 <td> 20 <td> 49 <td> 9 <tr>
<td> June <td> 73 <td> 23 <td> 55 <td> 13 <tr>
<td> July <td> 76 <td> 24 <td> 58 <td> 14 <tr>
<td> August <td> 75 <td> 24 <td> 58 <td> 14 <tr>
<td> September <td> 76 <td> 24 <td> 53 <td> 12 <tr>
<td> October <td> 60 <td> 16 <td> 46 <td> 8 <tr>
<td> November <td> 50 <td> 10 <td> 40 <td> 4 <tr>
<td> December <td> 44 <td> 7 <td> 36 <td> 2 <tr>
</table>
```

Figure 4-7. Server definition of a table

# Temperatures

Average daily maximum and minimum temperatures

| Month | Max (F) | Max (C) | Min (F) | Min (C) |
|-----------|---------|---------|---------|---------|
| January | 43 | 6 | 34 | 1 |
| February | 45 | 7 | 34 | 1 |
| March | 54 | 12 | 39 | 4 |
| April | 60 | 16 | 43 | 6 |
| May | 68 | 20 | 49 | 9 |
| June | 73 | 23 | 55 | 13 |
| July | 76 | 24 | 58 | 14 |
| August | 75 | 24 | 58 | 14 |
| September | 76 | 24 | 53 | 12 |
| October | 60 | 16 | 46 | 8 |
| November | 50 | 10 | 40 | 4 |
| December | 44 | 7 | 36 | 2 |

Figure 4-8. Browser display of a table

You can use a spreadsheet to speed up the preparation of a table definition. For example, the table definition shown in Figure 4-7 was created by setting up a spreadsheet with 11 columns (see Figure 4-9). After entering the **<td>** and **<tr>** tags in the second row, use the fill down command to enter the remaining tags. Then, complete the data entry and cut-and-paste the table into your editor. Of course, we were extra smart in this case. We used a formula to convert Fahrenheit to Celsius.

| <th> | Month | <th> | Max (F) | <th> | Max(C) | <th> | Min(F) | <th> | Min(C) | <tr> |
|------|-------|------|---------|------|--------|------|--------|------|--------|------|
| <td> | January | <td> | 4 3 | <td> | 6 | <td> | 3 4 | <td> | 1 | <tr> |
| <td> | February | <td> | 4 5 | <td> | 7 | <td> | 3 4 | <td> | 1 | <tr> |
| <td> | March | <td> | 5 4 | <td> | 1 2 | <td> | 3 9 | <td> | 4 | <tr> |
| <td> | April | <td> | 6 0 | <td> | 1 6 | <td> | 4 3 | <td> | 6 | <tr> |
| <td> | May | <td> | 6 8 | <td> | 2 0 | <td> | 4 9 | <td> | 9 | <tr> |
| <td> | June | <td> | 7 3 | <td> | 2 3 | <td> | 5 5 | <td> | 1 3 | <tr> |
| <td> | July | <td> | 7 6 | <td> | 2 4 | <td> | 5 8 | <td> | 1 4 | <tr> |
| <td> | August | <td> | 7 5 | <td> | 2 4 | <td> | 5 8 | <td> | 1 4 | <tr> |
| <td> | September | <td> | 7 6 | <td> | 2 4 | <td> | 5 3 | <td> | 1 2 | <tr> |
| <td> | October | <td> | 6 0 | <td> | 1 6 | <td> | 4 6 | <td> | 8 | <tr> |
| <td> | November | <td> | 5 0 | <td> | 1 0 | <td> | 4 0 | <td> | 4 | <tr> |
| <td> | December | <td> | 4 4 | <td> | 7 | <td> | 3 6 | <td> | 2 | <tr> |

Figure 4-9. Using a spreadsheet for table definition

## Forms

Interactive Web applications can be created using HTML's form definition commands. Although it is very easy to create a form, processing it requires considerably more skill because each form needs a corresponding application to process its data. When a completed form is submitted, the data are sent to the Web server, which simply passes the data on to an application specifically built for handling the form (see Figure 4-10). After processing the data, the form handler returns a response to the Web server (e.g., Thank you for your order), which is then sent to the browser for display. A form handler application is written using a language such as C++. Because you need programming skills to process forms, we will not cover the HTML for forms design.

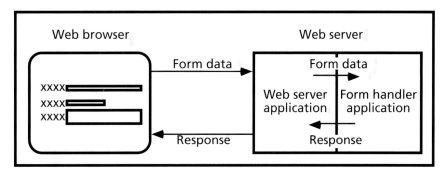

Figure 4-10. Processing a form

## Maps

A map is an interesting alternative to a menu of links. Instead of clicking on the text of a link, the user clicks on a region of an image, which can be rectangular, circular, oval, or irregular. Any image can be converted to an active map. Because a map is graphically active, the coordinates of the point clicked are used to determine the action to be taken, such as linking to another page.

Maps can be processed by the server or the client. When first introduced, maps required map processing software on the server to determine the appropriate action. Netscape 2.0 introduced client-side image maps, which means processing is handled by the browser. Although we discuss these two methods as both are currently used, we expect that client-side processing will quickly replace server-side processing, because it is faster and reduces network traffic and is likely to be adopted by other browsers.

**Server-side map processing.** Defining a map requires specifying the URL of the map processing application, the name of the map definition file, and adding the **ismap** key word to the img command, as shown:

```
<a href="mapserve.acgi$paris.map"><img
    src="parismap.gif" ismap></a>
```

When you click the mouse on a region of a map (parismap.gif in the preceding example), the browser sends the server the coordinates of the mouse's pointer. The server then passes these coordinates to the map processing application (mapserve.acgi), which determines the action to take based on the coordinates received (see Figure 4-11).

A map application requires a map definition file (paris.map in the preceding example), which defines the active regions of a map. A map definition file is a text file containing a line for each region. For rectangular regions, the line contains the top left and bottom right coordinates. For a circular region, the line contains the coordinates of the center and one edge to determine the radius of the circle. Ovals are defined by the rectangle that bounds them. Irregular regions are described by the x,y coordinates for each vertex. The coordinates of a region on a map can be readily determined using special software that displays the coordinates of any point on a graphic. The top-left corner of a map is defined as (0,0), and each pixel represents one coordinate unit (see Figure 4-12).

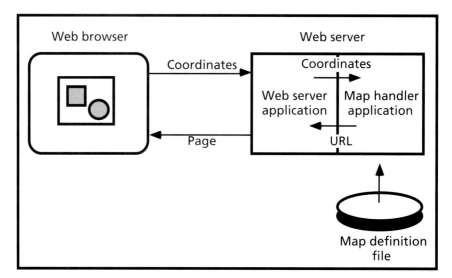

Figure 4-11. Processing a map

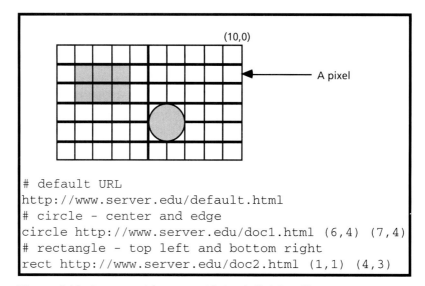

```
# default URL
http://www.server.edu/default.html
# circle - center and edge
circle http://www.server.edu/doc1.html (6,4) (7,4)
# rectangle - top left and bottom right
rect http://www.server.edu/doc2.html (1,1) (4,3)
```

Figure 4-12. A server-side map with its definition file

**Client-side map processing.** Map definition requires adding the **usemap** keyword to the **img** command and defining the map within a HTML document. The data for defining the map (the map in Figure 4-12 is also used for this example) is contained within the **map** element. Each map has a **name**. In the example in Figure 4-13, the HTML segment **<map name="parismap">** declares the name of the map. Notice that for the **img** element, the same name appears following the **usemap** keyword. It is preceded by # because it is a link within the document (see page 85). The image and map need not be within the same document, in which case a full URL is required (e.g., usemap="http://www.server.edu/ maps.html#parismap").

```
<img src="parismap.gif" usemap="#parismap">
<map name="parismap">
<!-- define a circle by its center and radius    -->
<area shape="circle" coords="6,4,1" href="doc1.html">
<!-- define a rect by its upper left              -->
<!--                    and lower right            -->
<area shape="rect" coords="1,1,4,3" href="doc2.html">
</map>
```

Figure 4-13. HTML for client-side map processing

A **map** element must contain **area** elements that define the regions of an image and the linked reference. Circles, rectangles, and polygons are the supported regions. For example, clicking within the rectangular region bounded on the top left by (1,1) and the bottom right by (4,3) will result in a relative link to doc2.html. If necessary, the **href** can be a full URL. Observe that the method of defining a client-side map is slightly different from that for a server-side map (e.g., circles are defined differently).

## Frames

As we discussed in Chapter 3, one of the enhancements in Netscape 2.x and 3.x is the capability to work with **frames**. Recall that a frame is a section of the Netscape window in which a Web page can be displayed. It is possible with HTML to create frames with the **<frameset>** and **<frame>** tags. The **<frameset>** tag defines the number and form of the frames to be created, and the **<frame>** tag defines what will be displayed in each frame. It is important to note that the HTML document that creates frames is usually very simple since its primary purpose is to create the form of the frames page and to refer to other Web pages that will be displayed in the frames.

The general form of a frames page is similar to that of a nonframes Web page except that the **<body>** tag is replaced by the **<frameset>** tag. The general form of a frames page with two horizontal frames is shown in Figure 4-14. In this case, the top horizontal frame named "window1", takes up the top 33 percent of the screen and contains a page with the file name "banner.htm". The lower horizontal frame, named "window2", takes up the bottom 67 percent of the screen and contains a page with the file name "home2.htm". These two pages must be created separately using the HTML tags discussed earlier. The *scrolling* parameter in the first frame indicates that it should not have a scroll bar; otherwise, one will be added if needed. If you wanted to create a Web page with vertical frames, you would use the *cols* parameter instead of *rows*.

The result of this HTML code is shown in Figure 4-15 (where banner.htm and home2.htm are the files used to create the UGA Swim Team frames Web page discussed in Chapter 3).

```
<html>
<head>
<title>Frames Web Document</title>
</head>
<frameset rows = "33%,67%">
<frame name="window1" src= banner.htm scrolling =
"no">
<frame name="window2" src= home2.htm>
</frameset>
</html>
```

Figure 4-14. HTML for a frame

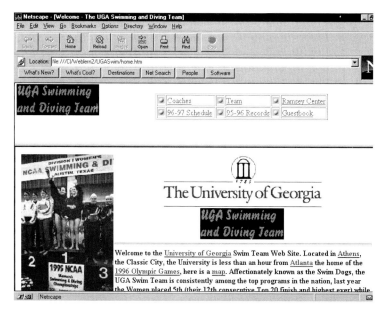

Figure 4-15. Result of HTML for a frame

*Special characters*

You have already seen some examples of special characters in HTML (e.g., é in Métro). These special characters are defined using the general format &charactername; where charactername is descriptive of the character (e.g., &eacute; for é). Note the use of & and ; to indicate the beginning and end of the definition of a special character. Because &, <, and, > have a special meaning within HTML, these characters must be represented as special characters (see Table 4-18). Appendix A contains a complete listing of special characters.

Table 4-19: Some special characters

| Server | Browser |
|--------|---------|
| &amp; | & |
| &lt; | < |
| &gt; | > |
| &eacute; | é |

## Your Turn!

1. Create a Web page using HTML that will display a table of the following currency exchange rate information for $1 US. Save this Web page as a:\currency.htm

| Country | Currency | Exchange rate |
|---------|----------|---------------|
| Australia | Dollar | 1.29 |
| United Kingdom | Pound | .65 |
| Canada | Dollar | 1.37 |
| France | Franc | 5.03 |
| Germany | Mark | 1.48 |
| Japan | Yen | 106.00 |
| Mexico | Peso | 7.51 |
| Spain | Peseta | 126.00 |

2. Create a Web page with horizontal frames that will display the currency Web page you created in Exercise 1 in the top frame and the last version of docnum1.htm created in earlier exercises in the lower frame. Make the frames of equal size (50 percent each) and allow both of them to scroll if necessary.

## Using Netscape Gold

With the increasing popularity of the World Wide Web, more and more people want to create Web pages. Netscape Gold is a version of the Netscape Navigator that is aimed at helping you create Web pages. It does this by incorporating an editor into the browser. However, unlike your usual editor, you do not need to enter HTML tags; what you see is what you get. The Netscape Gold editor takes care of that for you. When you have created a Web page in the editor, the page appears much as it will when you view it on the Web. In addition, by clicking on a button, you can jump into the browser and see exactly how it will appear.

**Hints for creating Web sites**

As more and more individuals and organizations are creating Web sites, it becomes increasingly important to understand what makes a Web site attract visitors. Here are some hints on creating Web sites from Andrew B. King, a partner in Athenia Associates, a company devoted to creating high-content, high-traffic Web sites. He makes suggestions in three areas: content, form, and interactivity.

1. Your Web site should reflect the culture of the Web, which means you should have something valuable to give to your visitors: information, software, advice, humor, and so on. Original content is the most important trait of a great Web site. Don't make your site just a list of links to other sites; find a niche and dominate it.

2. Web sites should be updated frequently to avoid staleness and be well-edited for readability. They should also use graphics sparingly and should be designed for quick downloading. Make sure your site is well-organized; that is, balance the number of levels with page length to minimize scrolling and display time. Finally, your site should use appropriate metaphors for your interface. For example, the Zima beverage site uses a fridge as its metaphor.

3. Your Web site should be interactive—it should allow your visitor to interact with the site through forms, e-mail, or some other type of interactivity. This should include self-generating content that allows your visitors to share information with others and to shape your site to their needs.

Adapted from King, A. B. What makes a great Web site? *Navigate!* June 1996.

Netscape Gold can be accessed by clicking on the appropriate icon on the Windows screen. The Netscape Gold icon is very similar to the Netscape browser icon except that it has a gold hue to it. Once you access Netscape Gold, the screen will appear exactly like the browser screen with the exception of an additional toolbar button—the Edit button. If you click on the Edit button or the **File | New Document** or **File | Edit Document** options, the Netscape Gold editor screen is displayed. This is a blank screen with a series of toolbars that are used to create the Web page. These toolbars are shown in Figure 4-16.

The buttons on the Netscape Gold toolbars enable you to create a Web page by pointing and clicking. Each button has a descriptive picture and, if you position the mouse pointer over a button, a descriptive ToolTip pops up. For example, in Figure 4-16, the mouse pointer is positioned over the toolbar button with a horizontal line on it, and the resulting ToolTip indicates that clicking on this button will place a horizontal line on the Web page. So, instead of using the **<hr>** code to create a horizontal line, you simply click this

Figure 4-16. Netscape Gold editor toolbars

button. In addition to the toolbar buttons, the menu bar has Insert and Properties options that enable you to insert new features in the Web page or to modify existing features.

Two toolbar buttons of particular interest are the browser and publish buttons. The **browser button** is used to switch from the Netscape Gold editor to the browser function. When you click this button, the Web page created in Gold is displayed in the browser in the form in which it will be displayed on the Web. On the other hand, the **publish button** is used to create the actual Web page on a server computer. It does this by saving all text and image files that are a part of the Web page to the server. They must be saved to a local hard disk first to be published.

There is not sufficient space in this textbook to cover the Netscape Navigator Gold editor in depth, but if you have Netscape Gold or are interested in using it, a dedicated Web site[3] and complete tutorial[4] are available.

## Key terms and concepts

| | |
|---|---|
| absolute addressing | logical style |
| anchor tag | map |
| browser | multimedia |
| browser button | physical style |
| client-side map | publish button |
| comments | relative addressing |
| form | server |
| frames | server-side map |
| hyperlink | special character |
| hypermedia | style tag |
| hypertext markup language (HTML) | table |
| image | tag |

---

3. http://home.netscape.com/home/starter.html

4. http://home.netscape.com/eng/mozilla/3.0/handbook/

# Exercises

1. Create a page describing yourself. Make certain you include the capability for people to send you e-mail.

2. Add some links from your home page to some of your favorite Web sites.

3. Modify your home page so that you can link to text within it (i.e., try linking within a document).

4. Write a description of a friend. Use appropriate logical styles to emphasize some key attributes of your friend. Using appropriate HTML coding, include a common phrase or remark you often hear your friend say.

5. Pretend that you are a famous writer of detective novels. Write a description of yourself, and include the names and details of two books you have written. Use headings to separate the different parts of the text.

6. Two other HTML styles are center and blink. Write HTML code to discover the effect of these commands. (Hint: The first pair of each the tags are **<center>** and **<blink>**, respectively.)

7. Create a standard set of HTML code to be placed at the bottom of each document you create.

8. Strikethrough, superscript, and subscript are physical styles with leading tags **<s>**, **<sup>**, and **<sub>**, respectively. Write HTML to investigate how text formatted with these styles is displayed.

9. Write HTML to list the names of five capital cities in Europe.

10. The five largest cities in France are: Paris 2,152,000; Marseilles 801,000; Lyon 415,000; Toulouse 359,000; Nice 342,000 (1990 estimates). Write HTML to show these cities ranked by size; display the population as well as the city's name.

# 5    Advanced browsing

- - - - - - - - - - - - - - - - - - - - - - - - - - - - - - - - -

**Objectives**

After completing this chapter, you will be able to:

- ❖ use Web search engines and directories;
- ❖ use other Internet resources in conjunction with the Web;
- ❖ describe the major methods of electronic information exchange.

**Introduction**

In earlier chapters, you learned the basics of Web navigation using Web documents stored on a local disk. Now it is time to leave the nest and venture onto the Web itself for some advanced browsing. In this chapter, you will access Web sites throughout the world. The URL of each mentioned site is listed in a footnote. To make life easier, all of these sites, and some other interesting places, are listed at one Web site.[1] Thus, you can type the URL of each site or connect to the central listing.

**Finding Web resources**

By now you will have realized that the Web contains a tremendous variety of useful information. But how do you find things? Fortunately, because all Internet resources are stored in electronic format, we can use computers to help us search for information.

---

1. http://www.negia.net/webbook

**Surfing the Net for a job**

As college students approach the end of their senior year, most are either looking for a job or considering graduate school. In either case, the Net is providing an improved way of reaching their goal. For those students who are entering the job market, there are several Web sites that are dedicated to electronically pairing job applicants with organizations that are actively searching for new employees. You will probably want to visit one of these Web sites as a part of your overall job search. One of the most ambitious of these job-hunting sites is JobDirect which tries to pair entry-level workers with prospective employers by matching the job-searcher's skills and areas of interest with those of employers. JobDirect has an on-line resumé writing service and a job database which the job-seeker can search for free.

Other Web sites aimed at helping job-seekers find positions include JobWeb which is maintained by the National Association of Colleges and Employers and E-span. JobWeb contains thousands of job postings as well as links to many other career-oriented Web sites. E-span offers the capability to search its listings with keywords and to post your resumé in its ResumePro Database. For those who want to search the want-ads from multiple big-city newspapers, CareerPath is the site to visit with a compilation of classified ads from nine newspapers including the *Boston Globe* and *New York Times*.

For those graduating students who are considering graduate school, it is a good idea to search the Web to determine if the universities which you are considering have a Web site; most do. Many schools are now offering the capability for prospective students to view course offerings, faculty research, and a wealth of information on the school and its environs. Some schools such as Penn State are even making it possible to apply and be accepted via Web forms and e-mail.

Adapted from: Weiss, A., Grad seeks job. *Internet World.* September 1996: 76-79; and Colleges scout for students on the Net. *Athens Banner-Herald.* April 1, 1996: 6.

*Note:* The URLs for the sites mentioned above can be found on the support Web site (http://www.negia.net/webbook).

*Directory buttons*

Netscape's **Directory buttons** (see Figure 5-1), which were briefly mentioned in Chapter 3, are a good place to start when seeking information. Each of these buttons is now discussed. Remember, you will need Web access to explore personally any of these buttons.

Figure 5-1. Directory buttons

What's New
: The What's New page, maintained by Netscape, lists some recent additions that illustrate advanced features of the Web or are particularly innovative. The explosive growth of the Web means that this can be only a sample of new pages. If you are looking for imaginative and resourceful uses of the Web, this is a good place to start.

What's Cool?
: What's Cool is a list of pages that Netscape classifies as cool. As Shakespeare might have said: "Methinks cool is in the brain of the browser." Again, if you are looking for some fresh ideas, check out What's Cool.

Destinations
: Destinations is a showcase of browser technology. It provides links to sites using the last helper applications and plug-ins, and advanced use of Java. This is a good place to visit to remain abreast of Web technology innovations.

Net Search
: Net Search accesses a list of search engines and directories, which are used for finding Web pages. Searching is covered in more detail in the next section.

People
: Finding a person's Internet address is not as simple as dialing the telephone company's directory service or flipping through the telephone book. Because the Internet is a loose federation of networks, there is no central registry of addresses. Fortunately, the Internet contains several databases that house information about individuals. The people button provides access to a range of electronic directories.

Software
: Clicking on the Software button takes you to Netscape's product page, where you can register your copy of Netscape, upgrade to a later release, or download components. If you are a regular user of Netscape's browser, then it is a good practice to visit this page frequently to find out what's new. Netscape and other software suppliers are continually adding features and plug-ins.

## Finding information

There are two approaches to finding information on the Web: use a search engine or directory. A simple analogy will help you understand the difference between a search engine and a directory. Imagine you arrive in a city that you have never visited before. You have to travel to the other side of the city and have two choices: take a cab or rent a car. Taking a cab is like using a search engine. You hop in the cab and give the driver the address of where you would like to go. In the case of searching, you give the search engine some keywords that identify the pages of interest. If you are sufficiently precise, you should locate a small number of highly relevant pages. The computer, like the cab driver, handles navigation. Renting a car is like using a directory. You use a map to find your way. With a directory, you follow a hierarchical structure of topics to a set of relevant pages. As with renting a car, you are responsible for navigation.

Searching works well when you can specify appropriate keywords. It is a good idea to start with a search engine and if that fails, use a directory. The advantage of a directory is that the hierarchical structure provides guideposts to help you in your search. A directory is especially useful when you cannot seem to find keywords for your search.

Searching

Imagine you are planning a vacation in Bermuda and would like to read some tourist information before deciding where to stay and what to do. Try using Net Search, which gives you access to a variety of **search engines**. The list of search engines is in two parts: a series of buttons at the top and links at the bottom (see Figure 5-2). As search engines vary in their speed and usefulness, it pays to experiment and find the one that you prefer.

Figure 5-2. Net Search options

After selecting a search engine, enter the keywords *bermuda tourist information* (see Figure 5-3). A successful search returns a list of Web sites matching the keywords. In this case, the partial results of the search (see Figure 5-3) provide links to two Web sites containing tourist information. Another couple of clicks and you will be in Bermuda—virtually. Happy holiday!

There are a number of search engines available. If you find one is slow because of Web traffic or it does not give you a relevant list of pages, then try one of the others reached via the Net Search button. Some search tools have additional helpful features. For example, Magellan gives you a choice of searching rated and reviewed sites or the entire database. A search of rated and reviewed sites should be faster and maybe avoid reporting home pages

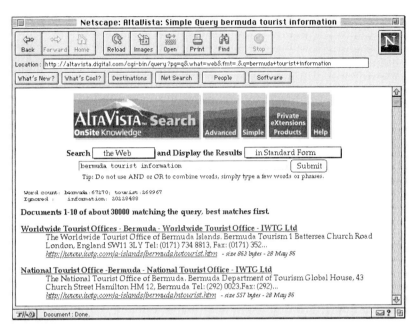

Figure 5-3. A search request and partial results

in which you have no interest (e.g., Fred Blogg's report on his Bermuda vacation). On the other hand, there may be pages that Magellan has not rated and are of potential interest. If you elect to search only rated and reviewed sites, you will miss these. It's a good idea to store your favorite search engines as bookmarks. This will save you from accessing the often busy Netscape server.

As more and more documents are stored on the Web, finding relevant information requires greater precision. For example, if you used only the keyword *bermuda,* most of the pages found by the search engine would be irrelevant. By using the three keywords (*bermuda tourist information*), you narrow the search to the domain of interest. Select your search words carefully to limit the search to what is relevant to your current needs.

**Searching tips**   Not all search engines work the same way, but there are some basic search specification concepts that should work for your favorite search engine. Also, some search engines (e.g., Alta Vista) have a **simple mode** and an **advanced mode**. Queries that use the binary operators AND, OR, NEAR and the unary operator NOT should be used with the advanced search mode; otherwise they may be treated as search words and not operators.

Some common approaches to specifying searches are:

❖ A simple keyword search
    rock music
will identify pages containing *either* the word "rock" or "music."

❖ Boolean query
    rock AND music
will identify pages containing *both* the words "rock" and "music."

❖ Phrase query
   "rock music"
will identify pages containing the entire phrase "rock music."

❖ Complex query
   Elvis AND "rock music"
will identify pages containing the word Elvis and the phrase "rock music."

❖ Complex query
   rock AND NOT music
will identify pages containing the word "rock" and not containing the word "music."

❖ Proximity query
   Fred NEAR Bloggs
will find those pages where the words "Fred" and "Bloggs" are within ten
   words of each other. This query will find pages containing *Fred Bloggs,*
   *Fred Tom Bloggs, Fred T. Bloggs,* and *Bloggs, Fred.*

❖ Other advanced features
   An advanced query function will often offer other options, such as indicating the order in which found documents should be reported and a range
for the date of documents to be reported (see Figure 5-4).

Figure 5-4. An advanced search with Alta Vista

If your search does not produce many relevant documents, try some of the following tactics:

❖ read the help screens and searching tips for the search engine;

❖ specify the search more precisely;

❖ use AND to narrow the search (OR will broaden it);

❖ try another search engine.

**Net Directory**    As discussed previously, an alternative search strategy is to use a directory. Many of the search engines also have a parallel directory structure. Yahoo!,[2] perhaps the most famous directory, lists Web sites by major categories (e.g., business), with each category further broken down into subcategories (e.g., marketing) which may be further subdivided into topics (see Figure 5-5).

Figure 5-5. Yahoo's major categories

Let's say you have an all-abiding interest in Australian Rules Football (the game for real men without helmets and padding). You can use Yahoo! to find home pages dealing with this subject. The major category is Recreation, subcategory Sports, and topic Football (Australian). If you follow this path, you will learn that 1996 is the centennial of that great Aussie game of footy.

---

2. http://www.yahoo.com/

**Tactics for keeping current**

It is impossible for anyone to keep track of Web development. There are just too many new pages being added and many existing pages are continually being revised. The great advantage of the Web—the ease with which pages can be created and maintained—also causes two major problems. First, how do you find information? Second, how do you make certain people can find your home page?

The first problem was addressed earlier in this section. Use search engines or directories to find pages that match your interests. Once you have found pages that are likely to be of continuing interest, make them book-marks. For instance, if you are a sports fan, you might want to add ESPNet[3] to your list of bookmarks. Commonly used search engines and directories are also good candidates for bookmarks.

Once you have added a few **bookmarks**, you will find scanning of the bookmark list somewhat tedious. Fortunately, Netscape allows you to create a hierarchical directory of personal bookmarks. You can collect all your leisure interest pages, in alphabetical order, under the heading *Leisure*.

Getting people to find your home page, the second problem, is a particularly important issue for businesses. There is not much sense advertising on the Web if very few people visit your home page. As you would expect, there are several tools for registering your page with search engines and directories. Even better, there is a Web site that facilitates mass registration,[4] so that you can quickly transmit the URL and descriptive keywords of your page to the major search engines and directories. Registering your page is not just for organizations; anyone can do it. If you develop some pages describing a particular event (e.g., recorded sightings of Elvis) or hobby, then register it so that anyone else with a similar interest can find your work.

There are services that will automatically notify you when a Web page has changed. For example, URL-minder is an automatic web-surfing robot that keeps track of changes to Web pages that you have registered.[5] This is a surefire way to guarantee that you have the latest patches or utilities for your favorite software. Just sign up for e-mail notification whenever the software provider's page is altered. If you check the home page for this book,[6] you will find you can sign up to be alerted when the page is revised.

Another useful technique for keeping current is **Frequently Asked Questions—FAQs** (pronounced *facks*). Many Web visitors, and indeed some users of other software, often ask the same questions. Consequently, some Web sites keep track of these questions and list them with a corresponding response. Skimming through the FAQs is an efficient means of discovering the features and limitations of a Web site or a piece of software. Kodak uses FAQs to inform customer about its new Advanced Photo System.[7]

---

3. http://espnet.sportszone.com
4. http://www.submit-it.com/
5. http://www.netmind.com/
6. http://www.negia.net/webbook
7. http://www.kodak.com/ciHome/APS/FAQs.shtml

■ ■ ■ ■ ■ ■ ■ ■ ■ ■ ■ ■ ■ ■ ■ ■ ■ ■ ■ ■ ■ ■ ■ ■ ■ ■ ■ ■

## Your turn!

1. Use Net Search to find information on the place you would most like to visit on your next vacation.

2. Repeat the previous exercise, using Net Directory. Which search was more successful? How easy was it to use each tool?

3. What is the U.S. President's e-mail address?

4. What is Bill Gates's e-mail address? (Hint: He has something to do with Microsoft.)

5. Do a search for something of interest using a search engine and a directory. Which was more efficient? Why? Can you make a generalization?

■ ■ ■ ■ ■ ■ ■ ■ ■ ■ ■ ■ ■ ■ ■ ■ ■ ■ ■ ■ ■ ■ ■ ■ ■ ■ ■ ■

## The Web—the mother of all Internet resources

The Web is a general interface to many other Internet resources. For example, a Web browser can download FTP files. Thus, once you have learned how to use a Web browser, you have access to many other Internet resources. In this section, we describe some other Internet resources and illustrate how to use HTML to access these resources from within a Web application (see Figure 5-6) using a browser or from within a Web application, respectively. Specifically, this section covers e-mail, newsgroups, FTP, and telnet.

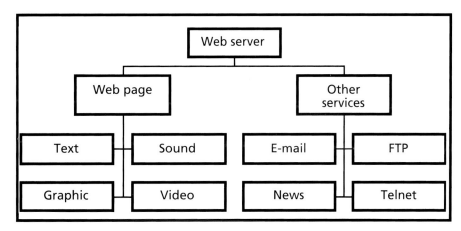

Figure 5-6. Web services

### Electronic mail

Second only to the Web in terms of Internet traffic, e-mail is an extremely popular use of the Internet. As mentioned earlier, Netscape has always had the capability to send outgoing e-mail through the use of the mailto: protocol. However, with the introduction of Netscape 2.0, the capability to use the full potential of e-mail was realized. Now, it is possible to both send and receive e-mail messages from within Netscape without need of having a separate e-mail client. In this short discussion of the Netscape e-mail client, we will concentrate on the most basic operations: sending and receiving e-mail messages. There are other operations which we encourage you to explore on your own.

Sending e-mail    As with most other operations in Netscape, there are several methods to send e-mail. All of these involve opening the Message Composition window. You can open this window using the mailto: protocol as discussed in Chapters 2 and 4, by selecting **File | New Mail Message** or **File | Mail Document**, or by opening the main Netscape Mail window. In this discussion, we will assume you have selected **File | New Mail Message** to open the Message Composition window. (If the **File | Mail Document** option is used, the URL for the current Web page is already entered in the message field and will act as a hypertext link if the message is read using the Netscape e-mail client.) Shortly, we will discuss using the main Netscape Mail window to send and receive e-mail. Regardless of how the Message Composition window is opened, there is a five-step process to sending e-mail:

1. Open Message Composition window.
2. Fill in the e-mail address of the recipient in the Mail To: field (already done if the mailto: protocol is used).
3. Fill in the subject of the e-mail (not required but useful).
4. Enter a message in the large text window.
5. Click the Send button.

The Message Composition window is shown in Figure 5-7 with an e-mail address, subject, and message filled in.

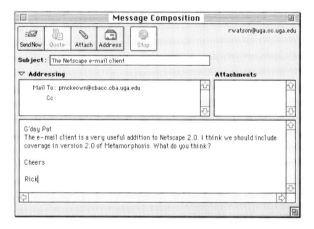

Figure 5-7. Netscape Message Composition window

Note that the Message Composition window has both a menu bar and a toolbar. The toolbar buttons cover most of the key operations involved in composing and sending a message. These buttons and their purpose are shown in Table 5-1.

Table 5-1: Toolbar buttons for Message Composition window

| Button | Purpose |
|--------|---------|
| Send | Transmit a completed message |
| Quote | Include the contents of the Web page as text in the e-mail message |
| Attach | Attach a file to an e-mail message that will be transmitted with the message |
| Address | Use an e-mail address from the user's address book |
| Stop | Stop transmitting the e-mail message |

Reading e-mail

To read e-mail, you must open the main Netscape Mail window. This can be done in one of two ways: clicking on the mail indicator envelope icon in the bottom right-hand corner of the Netscape browser screen or selecting Netscape Mail from the Window menu bar option. Recall from Chapter 3 that if there is an exclamation mark beside the mail indicator, then there is unread e-mail. In any case, the Netscape Mail window replaces the Netscape browser window. The mail window shows a list of your incoming messages, any folders you have created in which to store messages, and your first incoming message. Figure 5-8 shows the Netscape Mail window. Note that it is divided into three panes: in the upper left pane is the mailbox pane with a list of folders in which messages are stored. In the upper right frame is the message header pane which displays a list of the messages corresponding to the selected folder (Inbox in this case) in the mailbox pane. The bottom message pane displays the contents of the selected message (from Rick Watson) in the message header pane.

As with all Netscape windows, the mail window has a menu bar and a toolbar with buttons that represent the most commonly used operations. These include retrieving messages from the mail server, sending new mail, replying to or forwarding mail messages, navigating among mail messages, printing a mail message, and stopping the sending or retrieval process. These buttons and their operations are shown in Table 5-2.

In addition to the toolbar buttons, there are a few menu selections of which you should be aware. These menu selections are shown in Table 5-3 along with the action they carry out.

An important operation with the Mail window is managing your e-mail messages. Reading them is very easy: simply click on a message in the message header pane and the contents will appear in the bottom pane. However, once you have read a message, you will want to move it to a folder so that only new, unread messages appear in the message list. You may move a message from the message header pane by dragging it with the mouse to a folder in the mailbox pane or by using the **Message | Move** menu item. If you want to review a message in a folder, simply highlight the folder in the folder list and then click on the message.

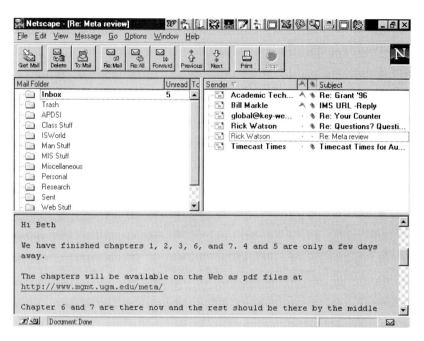

Figure 5-8. Netscape Mail window

Table 5-2: Toolbar buttons for Mail window

| Mail button | Operation |
| --- | --- |
| Get Mail | Retrieves messages from the mail server (usually done automatically when you go to the mail window) |
| Delete | Places a message in the Trash folder |
| To: Mail | Opens Message Composition window for a new mail message |
| Re: Mail (Re: All) | Opens Message Composition window with sender's address in Mail To: field (for Re: all button, all other recipient addresses are included) |
| Forward | Opens Message Composition window with this message attached for forwarding to someone else |
| Previous/Next | Moves highlighting to previous (next) unread message |
| Print | Prints the contents of the currently highlighted mail message |
| Stop | Stops retrieval or transmission of e-mail messages |

Table 5-3: Selected menu selections for the Mail window

| Menu selection | Action |
|---|---|
| File \| New Folder | Creates a new folder in which to store messages |
| Edit \| Delete Folder | Deletes the currently highlighted folder |
| Edit \| Delete | Deletes the currently highlighted message |
| View \| Sort | Controls the manner in which messages are sorted (by date, sender, subject, or message number) |
| Message \| Add to address book | Adds the e-mail address of sender to your address book |

**Discussion lists**

**Discussion lists** (also called **listservs**), another common use of the Internet, are built on e-mail facilities. An electronic meeting can easily be established for people with a common interest. Information exchange is facilitated by setting up an e-mail address to which any member of the group can send a message. The software then automatically distributes the message to everyone on the list. There are thousands of mailing lists. Some are very active with lots of traffic, and others are dormant. A list of publicly available mailing lists is maintained on the Web.[8] You can join any of them. There are also many private lists for which membership is controlled. For example, a firm may want to maintain a restricted list for communication with its major customers.

Be careful when replying to a message sent to a mailing list. The default is often to send a message to all subscribers, not just the person who originated the message. Failure to remember this procedure has frequently resulted in the embarrassment of a few and the amusement of many.

**News**

**News** is a vast set of discussion lists on a wide range of topics. **Newsgroups** are organized in a tree structure of discussion topics. While the number of top level categories varies with the news server to which you gain access, eight common major categories are shown in Table 5-4. A complete list of Newsgroups is available.[9]

News is based on a series of news servers that transfer messages to each other so that all postings to a newsgroup are replicated on all news servers. When a message is posted to a newsgroup on a particular server, it passes the message on to any news servers to which it talks. In this way, a message posted on one server eventually appears on all other servers.

Netscape 3.x and higher offers several ways of accessing Newsgroups. You can enter a URL with the news: protocol in the Location window (see Figure 5-9), or you can select the **Window \| Netscape News** menu item. In either case, the News window is displayed as shown in Figure 5-10. The only differ-

---

8. http://www.NeoSoft.com/internet/paml/

9. http://www.ph.tn.tudelft.nl/People/pierre/anchorman/Amn..html

Table 5-4: Common major news categories

| Category | Description |
|----------|-------------|
| alt | Alternative—just about anything that's not mainstream |
| comp | Computer science, software sources, and information on hardware and software systems (e.g., comp.databases) |
| misc | Topics not covered by the other categories (e.g., misc.forsale) |
| news | News network maintenance and software (e.g., news.admin.policy) |
| rec | Hobbies and recreation (e.g., rec.arts.cinema) |
| sci | Sciences (e.g., sci.astro.hubble) |
| soc | Social issues and social communications (e.g., soc.culture.australia) |
| talk | Discussion and debate on a variety of subjects (e.g., talk.politics.gun) |

ence in these two methods is that if you use the URL approach, the messages in this newsgroup are automatically displayed; otherwise, the News window opens showing only the news server to which you are subscribed. In Netscape 3.x, there is a default news group called, aptly enough, news. You can add additional servers through the **File I Open News Host** menu item.

Figure 5-9. Accessing a newsgroup using the location window

As with the Mail window, the News window has a menu bar, a toolbar, and three panes: a newsgroup pane, a message header pane, and a message pane. The menu bar and toolbar have many options that are similar to the Mail window, but we will not discuss them here. Click on an item in the newsgroup pane to display a listing of messages in the message header pane. Click on an item in the message header field to display each message in the message pane. If you wish to open a newsgroup that is not in the list, you can use the **File I Add Newsgroup** menu item and enter the name of the newsgroup. For example, to add the Lotus Notes discussion group to your list, simply select **File I Add Newsgroup** and enter comp.groupware.lotus-notes.misc. Note: Unless you subscribe to a newsgroup by clicking on the empty box to the right of it, this will be only a temporary addition to your list of Newsgroups.

If you wish to post a message on a newsgroup, simply click on the To: News button on the toolbar and fill in the information in the Message Composition window which appears. The address field has already been filled in with the newsgroup address.

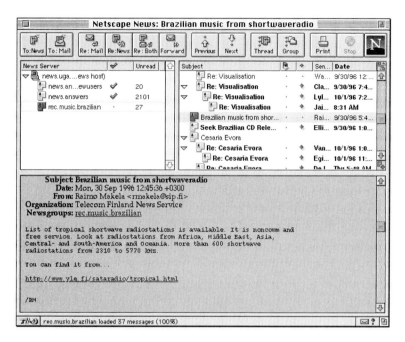

Figure 5-10. Netscape News window

While this is only a brief discussion of a very interesting topic, it should be enough to get you started. Remember, it is almost impossible, short of sending inappropriate messages, to go wrong with Newsgroups.

## Your turn!

1. What are the current hot topics for rec.backcountry?
2. ClariNet Communications Corporation publishes the ClariNet e.News, which appears as a major news category for many newsreaders. If your organization subscribes to the clari newsgroup, read the latest news from Australia (clari.world.oceania.australia).
3. What is the address of the newsreader for your organization? Is its address set for your browser?
4. Is there a newsgroup for Internet topics? What is it called? What topics are discussed by the members of this group?
5. What is the major difference between a discussion list and a newsgroup?
6. Send an e-mail message to bouncer@nic.near.net. You should receive a reply very quickly.
7. Subscribe to a discussion list and report what happens.

*FTP*

**FTP** (file transfer protocol) supports high-speed file transfer over the Internet. To make it easy to find the files you might want to copy, FTP also permits listing of directories. To transfer files, you generally need permission to access the host machine; however, because in many cases seeking approval would be burdensome and defeat the information sharing goal of the Internet, **anonymous FTP** is available, which opens a portion of a host's file space to all comers. Files are publicly available and may be copied. Many of the thousands of anonymous FTP hosts contain free software, shareware, and software upgrades. Some useful anonymous FTP sites are shown in Table 5-5.

Table 5-5: Some anonymous FTP sites

| Server | Company |
|---|---|
| ftp.microsoft.com | Microsoft |
| ftp.apple.com | Apple |
| ftp.adobe.com | Adobe |

Web browsers provide FTP support via the location window and HTML. The FTP address of a file or directory can be entered in the location window, as shown in Figure 5-11, where the main directory for Microsoft's anonymous FTP site is displayed. An anonymous FTP file can be retrieved from within a Web application by using a URL of the form (see also Table 5-6).

ftp://computer address:port/path.

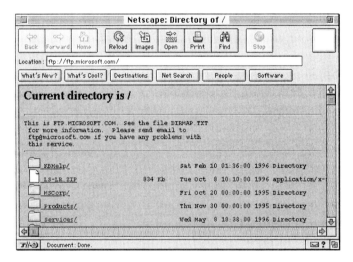

Figure 5-11. Accessing FTP using the location window

By specifying a URL that begins with ftp you can navigate directories, view files (including HTML and image files), and download and upload software. Netscape lets you access FTP servers in the same way you access Web servers. It will show the FTP directory, which usually includes the file's name, type, size, date, and possibly a short description. Icons are used to distinguish between directories (a folder) and files (a page). Clicking on a directory displays the subdirectory. There is usually a link at the top of the page that links to a higher level directory.

Clicking on a binary file downloads the software to your computer. When the download is complete, Netscape seeks a suitable helper application to open the file. For example, if the file has an extension of *pdf*, Netscape will launch Acrobat Reader to display the file. If the necessary helper application is not defined or available, a dialog box asks whether you want to save or discard the downloaded software.

Claris, for example, uses FTP to distribute trial versions of its software (you get to try it out for 30 days). The URL for downloading a trial version of Claris Works 4.0 for Windows is:

ftp://ftp.claris.com/pub/USA-Windows/Trial_Software/cw4trial.zip

If you specify a directory instead of a file, most browsers will give you a list of the directory's contents and allow you to select files or other directories. For example, to see all of Claris's trial versions, use:

ftp://ftp.claris.com/pub/USA-Windows/Trial_Software/

Table 5-6: FTP in HTML

| Server | Browser |
|---|---|
| `<a href="ftp://ftp.negia.net/webbook/specchrs.txt> Special character codes"></a>` | Special character codes |

## Your turn!

1. Use the location window of your browser to access the FTP site for this book (ftp.negia.net/webbook) and retrieve specchrs.txt.
2. Write HTML to provide FTP access to Claris's trial software.
3. Why is anonymous FTP useful?

## Telnet

**Telnet** is the main Internet protocol for connecting to a remote machine. It enables you to work on another computer on the Internet. Of course, you must have an authorized account on the other computer or be permitted to log in as an anonymous or general user. You can use telnet via the browser's location window or by coding HTML.

The HTML is fairly obvious, the service is *telnet,* and the address of the computer and port are specified. There is no need to indicate a path because you are trying to access a computer, not locate a file (see Table 5-7).

Incidentally, the telnet command shown in Table 5-7 connects you to a database listing information for cities in the United States and some interna-

Table 5-7: Telnet in HTML

| Server | Browser |
|---|---|
| `<a href = "telnet: //martini.eecs.umich.edu:3000/"> Geographic database server</a>` | Geographic database server |

tional locations. The database is searchable by city name, zip code, and so on; and reports data such as county, state, latitude and longitude, population, elevation, and zip code(s). Entering Athens, GA yields the output of Figure 5-12.

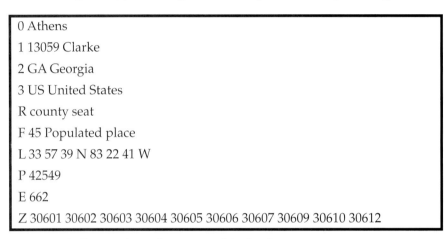

0 Athens

1 13059 Clarke

2 GA Georgia

3 US United States

R county seat

F 45 Populated place

L 33 57 39 N 83 22 41 W

P 42549

E 662

Z 30601 30602 30603 30604 30605 30606 30607 30609 30610 30612

Figure 5-12. Output from the geographic database server

## Your turn!

1. Using your Web browser, telnet to the geographic database and report the location of U.S. cities called Oslo. Also find Hell.

2. Check out whether you can telnet to your college or university's library and, if possible, do so.

## Netscape extensions

As you have already discovered, Netscape is more than a Web browser; it is a general-purpose tool for accessing Internet resources. In line with this idea, Netscape can be extended using helper applications and plug-ins, which make it possible to support playing audio and viewing videos, among other things.

Helper applications were the initial approach to extending Netscape. Helpers run applications or display files that aren't handled by Netscape. The file is displayed within the helper applications' window. Plug-ins, a more recent development, do not require a separate application to be launched because they are designed to work explicitly with the browser. Also, the file is displayed within Netscape's window. Both helpers and plug-ins can perform the same function (e.g., playing an audio file), but plug-ins are seamless.

Netscape has the built-in capability to read HTML code (as well as the GIF, JPEG, and XBM formats). Other file formats require the help of external helper applications or plug-ins. These file formats are organized according to MIME type (a method of differentiating file formats) so that when a file is retrieved from the server, Netscape can use a file's MIME type to determine how to handle it. For servers that do not provide a MIME type with a file, Netscape interprets the file's extension. For example, the html extension in the file name index.html indicates a file in HTML format.

**MIME.** Because people use a wide variety of operating systems, there is need for a common language that will enable the exchange of files that may include:

❖ non-ASCII character sets (e.g., Arabic or Kanji);

❖ special symbols (e.g., $\Sigma$);

❖ graphics;

❖ sounds;

❖ binary files (e.g., a spreadsheet).

**Multipurpose Internet mail extension (MIME)** is a widely used protocol for the interchange of files. The MIME protocol defines how the content of a document is mapped to a computer representation.

## *Helpers & plug-ins*

When Netscape encounters a file that it cannot process, it passes the data to the appropriate helper or plug-in for handling. A **helper** is an application program that Netscape loads to process the file (e.g., loading PowerPoint to display a file with a suffix of ppt). A **plug-in** functions as part of the Netscape program and is used like other built-in Netscape features. That is, there is no need to load an application. A plug-in provides seamless support for data types not supported by Netscape. A plug-in is installed on your hard disk where Netscape can find it (e.g., in the Plug-ins directory or folder).

Use **Options | General Preferences | Helpers** to access Netscape's Helpers dialog box in order to inspect whether a file's format maps to a helper or plug-in. The example shown in Figure 5-13 indicates that when a file with a suffix of vdo is received, VDOLine Player should be launched. (This handles streaming video.) The QuickTime plug-in handles QuickTime video. Netscape comes with some helpers and plug-ins predefined. You can reconfigure these and add new ones using the buttons on the right side of the screen. For example, the New button leads to a dialog box containing fields and buttons to specify MIME type, suffix, the helper application or plug-in, and associated action.

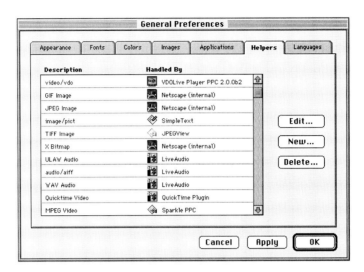

Figure 5-13. Helper and plug-in configuration

Macromedia's Shockwave is one plug-in you should consider installing because its Director software is widely used for creating animations.[10] Adobe's plug-in for reading pdf files is also very handy because of the widespread use of pdf (pdf is explained in the next section).[11] For a current list of plug-ins, check Netscape's list.[12]

## Electronic documents

The development of the Internet has created two important opportunities. First, people working in different parts of the world and for different organizations can just as readily collaborate as two people in the same firm working in adjacent offices. Second, anyone who has access to a Web server can become a publisher. Those with Web access can make their writings available to the world. Exploitation of these opportunities requires the capacity to share documents. At the simplest level, sharing can be done through simple text files; however, text files are a very inelegant solution because they are unformatted and do not support the exchange of graphics. Ideally, the reader of a shared document should see exactly the same image as the creator. There are two approaches to maintaining the image fidelity of the original document.

First, the author and the reader can synchronize their software. Both could agree to use the same word processor and, in some cases, to agree to use the same operating system. Then files can be exchanged using FTP or as attachments to e-mail messages. This approach is particularly useful for joint authorship of articles because all parties can read and amend the work. Forcing people to adopt the same word processor is not necessary, however, if the main goal is to share documents.

10. http://www.macromedia.com/shockwave/

11. http://www.adobe.com/acrobat/main.html

12. http://home.netscape.com/comprod/products/navigator/version_2.0/plugins/

The second approach is to use a common format for **electronic documents**. Ideally, what you would like to do is create an electronic copy of a document and share it. Two common approaches to creating electronic documents are Adobe's **portable document format (PDF)** and HTML.

---

### Going public over the Net

An event that many small or start-up businesses look forward to is going public. When a company goes public, it sells stock to the public in an initial public offering (IPO) to raise capital to expand its operations. This is often a very exciting event as the stock price is bid up by individuals anxious to invest in the company. However, as with almost all stock transactions, both the company and the investor have to work through a middleman. The company pays an investment banking firm to set up the public offering, and the investor pays a stockbroker to buy the stock. The cost of setting up the public offering through an investment bank often stands in the way of a small company going public. Once the stock is available to the public, it can be traded on a variety of stock exchanges, but as with the IPO, the buyers and sellers traditionally must work through stockbrokers to carry out the transactions.

However, the Net has the potential to structurally change both the IPO market and the stock market. The first use of the Net for an IPO came when Andy Klein decided to offer stock in his brewing company, Spring Street Brewing, to the public. Even though he was an investment banker himself, Andy decided to offer stock via the brewer's Web site in 1995, selling almost 850,000 shares at $1.85 a share in the first year of the offering raising nearly $1.6 million in capital. Realizing that his investors would need a way of trading their stocks, he created a special bulletin board system to allow them to buy and sell Spring Street stock without the need of a stockbroker. Called Wit-Trade after a popular Spring Street beer, the system was approved by the Security and Exchange Commission.

Following the success of the Wit-Trade system, Andy Klein announced the formation of a new company, Wit Capital Corporation, on April 2, 1996. This company is dedicated to arranging IPOs the same way that Spring Street Brewery was capitalized—on the Internet. It also plans to create a digital stock exchange for trading stocks and bonds. In all cases, the system will be structurally changed by the radical movement to trading securities over the Internet.

Adapted from: Zgodzinski, D. Home-brewed stock. *Internet World.* July 1996: 89-92.

---

*PDF*

**PDF** is a **page description language** that captures electronically the layout of the original document. Adobe's Acrobat Exchange software permits any document created by a DOS, Macintosh, Windows, or Unix application to be converted to PDF. Producing a PDF document is very similar to printing, except the image is sent to a file instead of a printer. The fidelity of the original document is maintained—text, graphics, and tables are faithfully reproduced when the PDF file is printed or viewed. PDF is an operating system independent and printer independent way of presenting the same text and images on many different systems.

PDF has been adopted by a number of organizations, including the Internal Revenue Service[13] for tax forms and the *New York Times*[14] for an eight-page summary of its newspaper. PDF documents can be sent as e-mail attachments, retrieved using FTP, or accessed from a Web application. To decipher a PDF file, the recipient must use a special reader, supplied at no cost by Adobe[15] for all major operating systems. In the case of the Web, you have to configure your browser to invoke the Adobe Acrobat reader whenever a file with the extension pdf is retrieved.

*HTML*

HTML is a **markup language**, which means it *marks* a portion of text as referring to a particular type of information (e.g., Important). HTML does not specify how this is to be interpreted; this is the function of the browser. Often the person using the browser can specify how the information will be presented. For instance, the Options menu of Netscape permits you to indicate the font and size for rendering pages. As a result, the reader can significantly alter the look of the page, which could have been carefully crafted by a graphic artist to convey a particular look and feel. Thus, the person viewing a page may see an image quite different from what the designer intended.

*HTML or PDF?*

The choice between HTML and PDF depends on the main purpose of the document. If the intention is to inform the reader, then there is generally less concern with how the information is rendered. As long as the information is readable and presented clearly, the reader can be given control of how it is presented. Alternatively, if the goal is to influence the reader (e.g., an advertisement) or maintain the original look of the source document (e.g, a newspaper or magazine), then PDF is the better alternative. The two formats coexist. A PDF document can include links to a HTML document, and vice versa. Also, a number of leading software companies are working on extensions to HTML that will give the creator greater control of the rendering of HTML (e.g., specifying the font to be used). As well, the recent release 3.0 of

---

13. http://www.irs.ustreas.gov/prod/forms_pubs/forms.html

14. http://nytimesfax.com/

15. http://www.adobe.com:80/Acrobat/Acrobat0.html

Acrobat is designed to work more closely with a HTML browser. To assist you make the decision between HTML and PDF, we have summarized the major differences in Table 5-8.

Table 5-8: HTML versus PDF

| HTML | PDF |
|---|---|
| A markup language | A page description language |
| HTML files can be created by a wide variety of software. Many word processors include an add-on to generate HTML | PDF files are created using special software sold by Adobe, which is more expensive than many HTML creator alternatives |
| Browser is often free | Viewer is free |
| Captures structure | Captures structure and layout |
| Can have links to PDF | Can have links to HTML |
| Reader can change presentation | Creator determines presentation |

## Your turn!

1. Search the Web for some useful or interesting applications of Adobe's Acrobat Exchange. Where would be a good place to start looking?
2. Describe some potential applications of electronic publishing.
3. Discuss the pros and cons of electronic versus paper publication.
4. Check out whether your e-mail package is MIME compliant. If so, exchange attached files with someone else in the class.

## MUDs— a frontier for exploration

The Internet does have an element of fun. **MUDs** (multiple user dungeons or dimensions) originated in the late 1980s as multiple-user, electronic versions of the game "Dungeons and Dragons." A virtual world populated by the players and their creations, a MUD is an ongoing drama with an electronically assembled cast exploring and interacting in cyberspace.

Particularly addictive for students, MUDs were banned in Australia because their introduction sparked a 25 percent increase in Internet traffic out of the country. Some universities have banned MUDs because they waste too many computing resources and student time. You have been warned! Be wary of MUDs consuming your time. As you would expect, a list of MUD home pages is on the Web.[16]

---

16. http://www.cis.upenn.edu:80/~lwl/mhome.html

Today's MUDs may be prototypical of virtual worlds that will appear in the future. These worlds will move beyond the constrained text interchange of present MUDs to become multimedia. They may also become vehicles for social interaction. A MUD could be an ideal way for an organization to develop team spirit in a group that never meets face-to-face. Teams need play time if they are to develop the social bonding that is a precursor to goal commitment and successful project implementation. Many teams develop their social dimension outside of formal work assignments. For example, a team might lunch together after a meeting. Virtual teams, those formed by electronic links, need to find ways to socialize, and a MUD might be a convenient way of electronically developing a cohesive team.[17]

## Your turn

1. Who is in charge of the MUD called Envy? (Hint: Check out the Web site describing MUDs.)

## Key terms and concepts

| | |
|---|---|
| advanced mode search | MIME |
| anonymous FTP | MUD |
| bookmark | multipurpose Internet mail exte |
| discussion list | news |
| Directory button | newsgroups |
| e-mail | page description language |
| electronic document | PDF |
| FAQs | plug-in |
| FTP | proximity query |
| helper application | search engine |
| listserv | simple mode search |
| markup language | telnet |

17. For an expanded discussion of MUDs and their organizational application, see M. O. Devereaux and R. Johansen. *Bridging distance and diversity: navigating the challenges of distributed and cross-cultural business teams.* Menlo Park, CA: the Institute for the Future, 1993.

# 6    Electronic commerce fundamentals

- - - - - - - - - - - - - - - - - - - - - - - - - - - - - - - - - - - - -

**Objectives**

After completing this chapter, you will be able to:

- ✤ define and give examples of electronic commerce;
- ✤ understand the main features of the technology that makes electronic commerce feasible;
- ✤ define the major reasons for using electronic commerce;
- ✤ understand that electronic commerce is a business revolution;
- ✤ identify which organizations are prime candidates for the Web;
- ✤ describe three topologies for electronic commerce;
- ✤ describe security techniques for controlling access and protecting messages;
- ✤ discuss the four major options for electronic money.

**Introduction**

The previous chapters have laid the foundation for understanding how to use the Web, write Web applications, and use other Internet tools. Now it is time to learn how to exploit the Internet, and the Web in particular, to improve organizational performance. In the introduction to the first chapter, we argued that organizations need to make a metamorphosis—they have to abandon existing business practices to create new ways of interacting with stakeholders. This chapter will provide you with the insights to understand how an organization can make the transformation from caterpillar to butterfly.

## Electronic commerce defined

Electronic commerce, in a broad sense, is the use of computer networks to improve organizational performance. Increasing profitability, gaining market share, improving customer service, and delivering products faster are some of the organizational performance gains possible with electronic commerce. Electronic commerce is more than ordering goods from an on-line catalog. It involves all aspects of an organization's electronic interactions with its **stakeholders**, the people who determine the future of the organization. Thus, electronic commerce includes activities such as establishing a Web page to support investor relations or communicating electronically with college students who are potential employees.

## Technology

Computers can only communicate with each other when they speak a common language or use a common communication protocol. **Transmission Control Protocol/Internet Protocol (TCP/IP)** is the communication network protocol used on the Internet. TCP/IP has two parts. TCP handles the transport of data, and IP performs routing and addressing.

### Data transport

The two main methods for transporting data across a network are circuit and packet switching. Circuit switching is commonly used for voice and package switching for data. The telephone system is an example of a circuit-switched network in which each link of a predetermined bandwidth is dedicated to a predetermined number of users for a period of time.

The Internet is a packet switching network. The TCP part of TCP/IP is responsible for splitting a message from the sending computer into packets, uniquely numbering each packet, transmitting the packets, and putting them together in the correct sequence at the receiving computer. The major advantage of packet switching is that it permits sharing of resources (e.g., a communication link) and makes better use of available bandwidth.

### Routing

Routing is the process of determining the path a message will take from the sending to the receiving computer. It is the responsibility of the IP part of TCP/IP for dynamically determining the best route through the network. Because routing is dynamic, packets of the same message may take different paths and not necessarily arrive in the sequence in which they were sent.

### Addressability

Messages can be sent from one computer to another only when every server on the Internet is uniquely addressable. The Internet Network Information Center (InterNIC) manages the assignment of unique IP addresses so that TCP/IP networks anywhere in the world can communicate with each other. An IP address is a unique 32-bit number consisting of four groups of decimal numbers in the range 0 to 255 (e.g., 128.192.73.60). Because IP numbers are difficult to remember, they are mapped to names via a Domain Name Server (DNS). Thus the IP address 128.192.73.60 is more easily remembered as *aussie.mgmt.uga.edu.* The exponential growth of the Internet will eventually result in a shortage of IP addresses, and the development of next-generation IP (IPng) is underway.

## *Infrastructure*

Electronic commerce is built on top of a number of different technologies. These various technologies created a layered, integrated infrastructure that permits the development and deployment of electronic commerce applications (see Figure 6-1). Each layer is founded on the layer below it and cannot function without it.[1]

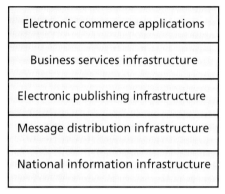

| Electronic commerce applications |
| Business services infrastructure |
| Electronic publishing infrastructure |
| Message distribution infrastructure |
| National information infrastructure |

Figure 6-1. Electronic commerce infrastructure

**National information infrastructure.** This layer is the bedrock of electronic commerce because all traffic must be transmitted by one or more of the communication networks comprising the national information infrastructure (NII). The components of an NII include the TV and radio broadcast industries, cable TV, telephone networks, cellular communication systems, computer networks, and the Internet. The trend in many countries is to increase competition among the various elements of the NII to increase its overall efficiency because it is believed that an NII is critical to the creation of national wealth.

**Message distribution infrastructure.** This layer consists of software for sending and receiving messages. Its purpose is to deliver a message from a server to a client. For example, it could move a HTML file from a Web server to a client running Netscape. Messages can be unformatted (e.g., e-mail) or formatted (e.g., a purchase order). Electronic data interchange (EDI), e-mail, and hypertext text transfer protocol (HTTP) are examples of messaging software.

---

1. This section is based on Applegate, L. M.; Holsapple, C. W.; Kalakota, R.; Rademacher, F. J.; Whinston, A. B. Electronic commerce: building blocks for new business opportunity. *Journal of Organizational Computing and Electronic Commerce.* 1996; 6(1): 1-10.

**Electronic publishing infrastructure.** Concerned with content, the Web is a very good example of this layer. It permits organizations to publish a full range of text and multimedia. There are three key elements of the Web:

❖ A uniform resource locator (URL), which is used to uniquely identify any server;

❖ A network protocol;

❖ A structured markup language, HTML.

Notice that the electronic publishing layer is still concerned with some of the issues solved by TCP/IP for the Internet part of the NII layer. There is still a need to consider addressability (i.e., a URL) and have a common language across the network (i.e., HTTP and HTML). However, these are built upon the previous layer, in the case of a URL, or at a higher level, in the case of HTML.

**Business services infrastructure.** The principal purpose of this layer is to support common business processes. Nearly every business, for example, is concerned with collecting payment for the goods and services it sells. Thus, the business services layer supports secure transmission of credit card numbers by providing encryption and electronic funds transfer. Furthermore, the business services layer should include facilities for encryption and authentication (see "Security" on page 140).

**Electronic commerce applications.** Finally, on top of all the other layers sits an application. Consider the case of a book seller with an on-line catalog (see Figure 6-2). The application is a book catalog; encryption is used to protect a customer's credit card number; the application is written in HTML; HTTP is the messaging protocol; and the Internet physical transports messages between the book seller and customer.

| | |
|---|---|
| Electronic commerce applications | *Book catalog* |
| Business services infrastructure | *Encryption* |
| Electronic publishing infrastructure | *HTML* |
| Message distribution infrastructure | *HTTP* |
| National information infrastructure | *Internet* |

Figure 6-2. An electronic commerce application

## Electronic commerce

Every business faces three strategic challenges: demand risk, innovation risk, and inefficiency risk.[2] Electronic commerce can be a device for reducing these risks.

### *Demand risk*

Sharply changing demand or the collapse of markets poses a significant risk for many firms. Smith-Corona, one of the last U.S. manufacturers of typewriters, recently filed for bankruptcy. Cheap personal computers have destroyed the typewriter market. In simple terms, **demand risk** means fewer customers want to buy a firm's wares. The globalization of the world market and increasing deregulation expose firms to greater levels of competition and magnify the threat of demand risk. To counter it, firms need to be flexible, adaptive, and continually searching for new markets and stimulating demand for their products and services.

The Web is global; millions of people have Web access, and this number is growing rapidly. Furthermore, many Web users are well-educated, affluent consumers—an ideal target for consumer marketing. Any firm establishing a Web presence, no matter how small or localized, instantly enters global marketing. The firm's message can be read by anyone with Web access. The South African wine retailer,[3] introduced in Chapter 1, can market to the entire Web world with a few pages on the Web. The Web levels the playing field. The economies of scale and scope enjoyed by large organizations are considerably diminished. So small producers do not have to negotiate the business practices of foreign climes in order to expose their products to new markets. They can safely venture forth electronically from their home base. Fortunately, the infrastructure—international credit cards (e.g., Visa) and international delivery systems (e.g., UPS)—for global marketing already exist. Add Web advertising and global marketing becomes a reality for many firms wherever they are located. Thus, the Web offers an excellent opportunity for reducing demand risk by diversifying into new markets.

A new medium for advertising, the Web enables firms to develop a home page where their products and services are described and promoted in considerable detail. Thousands of companies now have a Web presence, and in the foreseeable future nearly every company, from Fortune 500 giants, such as General Motors,[4] to small organizations such as Carroll EMC,[5] will be on the Web because it is a cheap and effective means of informing customers. For instance, for as little as $50 per month, a company can promote its wares on a commercial Web server.

A particular advantage of Web advertising is that it can be changed very quickly. Advertisements for traditional media—print, radio, and TV—are not as fortunate. For example, a glossy brochure may take weeks to prepare and

---

2. J. Child, Information technology, organizations, and the response to strategic challenges. *California Management Review,* Fall 1987: 33-50.

3. http://www.os2.iaccess.za/rhebok/index.htm

4. http://www.gm.com/

5. http://www.wgta.org/mempages/cemc/cemc.htm

distribute, and there is still the danger that many customers are referring to an older version. A Web home page can be updated easily and quickly, and customers always see the latest version. Web advertising means firms can react quickly to changing demand and adjust customer communication with alacrity.

Alternatively, firms can advertise on other Web sites. For example, EDS has an advertisement on the *What's New?* page of Netscape.[6] Because many people visit this Netscape page, the EDS message is highly visible. This form of advertising is very similar to using a billboard on a busy highway. The key to Web advertising, like most advertising, is to make the message visible to customers who are most likely to purchase. Thus, fast food outlets advertise on interstate highways because many passing customers need to stop for a meal. Similarly, firms who advertise on the Web must be certain that the *passing traffic* is likely to be interested in what they have to offer; otherwise the message is wasted and, even worse, irritating to possible customers. In most cases, Web advertising is simply a link, usually in the form of the company's logo, to a home page.

*Innovation risk*

Failure to be as innovative as competitors—**innovation risk**—is a second challenge. In an era of accelerating technological development, the firm that fails to continually improve its products and services is likely to lose market share to competitors and maybe even disappear. To remain alert to potential innovations, among other things, firms need an open flow of concepts and ideas. Customers are one particular source of innovative ideas because firms adapt and redesign products and services to meet their evolving needs. Thus, firms need to find efficient and effective means of continual communication with customers.

Internet communication (e-mail, lists, and news) can be used to create open communication links with a wide range of customers. E-mail can facilitate frequent communication with the most innovative customers. A list can be created to enable any customer to request product changes or new features. The advantage of a list is that another customer reading an idea may contribute to its development and elaboration. Also, a firm can monitor relevant newsgroups to discern what customers are saying about their products or services and those of competitors.

A firm can use the Web to pilot new ways of interacting with customers and other stakeholders. For example, it might experiment with different ways of marketing and delivering products and services. Or it can develop new communication channels with employees. Above all, firms need to be innovative in their use of the Web.

---

6. http://home.netscape.com/home/whats-new.html

*Inefficiency risk*

Failing to match competitors' unit costs—**inefficiency risk**—is the third strategic challenge. A major potential use of the Internet is to lower costs by distributing as much information as possible electronically. For example, instead of mailing out glossy brochures, a firm can create a Web site containing all the details of the brochure and more. Of course, it must notify customers of the address of its Web site, and this can be done in corporate advertising. Consequently, some companies (e.g., Toshiba) now list both a toll-free number and Web address in their print and TV advertisements.

The cost of handling orders can also be reduced by using interactive forms to capture customer and order information. Web ordering, compared to processing an order via a toll-free number, is estimated to be about a third of the cost. This saving results from the customers directly entering all data. Also, the firm can balance its work force because it no longer has to staff for peak phone ordering periods.

Consider the situation where a customer orders flowers via the Web (see Figure 6-3). In addition to entering delivery details, the customer can also specify special instructions and a message to appear on the card. Billing and credit card information (not shown in Figure 6-3) is also entered by the customer. Because the firm avoids this data entry, there are no misspellings of names or misunderstandings about delivery instructions or card message.

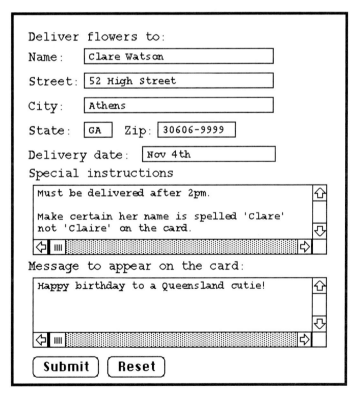

Figure 6-3. Ordering using the Web

## Your turn!

1. Visit General Motors and Carroll EMC (see footnotes 3 and 4 for the URLs). What similarities and differences do you note?

2. Find the Lands' End home page. Is it using the Web to reduce demand, innovation, or inefficiency risk?

## A business revolution

Electronic commerce using the Web is changing the nature of business because it levels the playing field and changes the direction of communication between buyers and sellers.

The Web provides a relatively level playing field for all participants in that:

❖ access opportunities are essentially equal for all players, regardless of size;

❖ share of voice is essentially uniform—no player can drown out others;

❖ initial setup costs are so low as to present minimal or nonexistent barriers to entry.

Small companies with a well-designed home page can look every bit as professional and credible as a large, multinational company (e.g., Flagpole Magazine[7]). Visitors can't tell if the business operates from a Manhattan sky-scraper or a garage. A small business can establish a Web presence for less than $50 per month and be just as accessible as the corporation spending $50,000 a month on its Web site. In traditional advertising media, the big corporation can dominate because it has more to spend. On the Web, no one can dominate because all Web pages are equally accessible.

Web advertising reverses the flow of communication. Instead of sending messages to customers, the firm now wants customers to converge on its home page. **Customer convergence** is the key to Web marketing. Unless customers find a firm's home page, the entire effort is wasted. This means a firm must ensure that its home page is found by any of the search engines a customer may elect to use. Even more, a firm with many products must ensure that potential customers converge on the page that describes the product or service of greatest potential interest. Thus, a camera manufacturer must first make certain that photography enthusiasts find its home page, and then help the potential customer, possibly with the aid of an expert system, navigate to the pages describing cameras or lenses of interest.

The shift from traditional broadcast advertising to customer convergence fundamentally changes the relationship between the advertiser and the customer, as summarized in Table 6-1. The initiative moves to the customer, who now decides which Web pages to view, and when they are viewed, what part of the message to read, and how the message is presented. For example, a cus-

---

7. http://www.negia.net/~flagpole/

tomer may decide to ignore an advertiser's message by never visiting its Web site, or disregard an important element of a message by turning off images and not playing audio clips.

Table 6-1: Communication flip-flop

| Traditional advertiser | Web customer |
|---|---|
| Decides audience | Decides advertiser |
| Decides schedule | Decides schedule |
| Decides message content | Selects and customizes content |
| Decides media for distribution | Decides how message is presented |

The **communication flip-flop** is a fundamental change in the nature of the relationship between buyers and sellers. As buyers increasingly use the Web to learn about new products and services, sellers will have to find ways of attracting visitors to their Web site and then enticing them to read their messages.

# Who should use the Web?

Each organization needs to consider whether it should have a Web presence, and if so, what should be the extent of its involvement. There are two key factors to be considered in answering these questions.

First, how many existing or potential customers are likely to be Web users? If a significant proportion of a firm's customers are Web users, then it should have a presence; otherwise it is missing an opportunity to inform customers of its products and services. The Web is user friendly and an extremely convenient source of information for many customers. If a firm does not have a home page, there is the risk that potential customers, attracted by the Web's ease of use, will flow to competitors who have a Web presence. Industrial marketers, companies that market to other businesses, are likely to find many of their customers already have access to the Web. Thus, it is not surprising to find that General Electric[8] has a significant Web presence. Another consumer segment with widespread access are advanced computer users, such as information systems specialists. Consequently, many of the hardware (e.g., DEC[9]) and software (e.g., Adobe[10]) firms have Web pages. Many college faculty, staff, and students have Web access, and most universities have home pages. Companies that recruit graduates, such as Andersen Consulting,[11] are likely to find that a Web presence is an effective communication medium (see page 102).

Second, what is the **information intensity** of a company's products and services? An information-intense product is one that requires considerable

---

8. http://www.ge.com:80/
9. http://www.digital.com/
10. http://www.adobe.com:80/
11. http://www.ac.com/careers/

133

information to describe it completely. For example, how do you describe a CD to a potential customer? Ideally, you would use text for the album notes and list the tunes, artists, and playing time; graphics to show the CD cover; sound for a sample of the music; and a video clip to show the artist performing. As you can see, a CD is information intensive because you need a great deal of information to describe it. Consequently, Sony Music[12] provides an image of a CD's cover, the liner notes, a list of tracks, and 30-second samples of some tracks. It also provides photos and details of the studio session.

Many industrial products (e.g., computers and chemicals) are information intensive. Du Pont Lubricants,[13] with its extensive data on the properties of krytox fluorinated oils, provides an excellent example of how the Web can efficiently deliver very detailed product information to customers.

The two parameters, number of customers on the Web and product information intensity, can be combined to provide a simple model (see Figure 6-4) for determining which companies should be using the Web. Organizations falling in the top-right quadrant are prime candidates because many of their customers have Web access and their products have a high information content. Firms in the other quadrants, particularly the lower-right quadrant, have less need to establish a Web site, although any company with high information content products and services should be gearing up for a significant Web presence because many of its customers probably surf the Net.

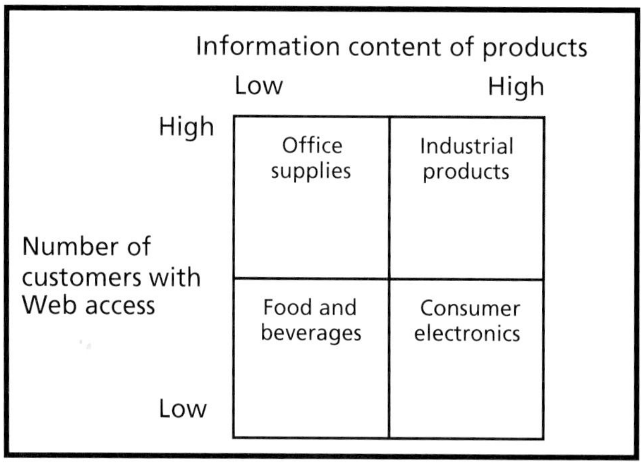

| Information content of products | |
|---|---|
| Low | High |
| Office supplies | Industrial products |
| Food and beverages | Consumer electronics |

Figure 6-4. Web presence grid with illustrative examples

Customers, of course, are not the only group with whom an organization may wish to communicate. Other stakeholders, those groups or individuals that can determine the future of an organization, can also be a communication target. Hence, some firms (e.g., MassMutual Consolidated[14]) use the Web to provide financial reports to investors or attract new employees (e.g.,

---

12. http://www.sony.com/Music/

13. http://www.lubricants.dupont.com:80/

14. http://www.massmutual.com/financial/finance.htm

Microsoft[15]). When many stakeholders have Web access, it becomes a general tool for communicating with them.

------------------------------------------------

## Your turn!

1. Visit DuPont Lubricant's page and note the level of detail provided.
2. How is Adobe using the Web to support customers?
3. Identify some organizations that are ideal candidates for the Web because their products have a high information content and many of their customers are likely to be Web users.

------------------------------------------------

## Electronic commerce topologies

There are three types of communication networks used for electronic commerce (see Table 6-2), depending on whether the intent is to support cooperation with a range of stakeholders, cooperation among employees, or cooperation with a business partner. Each of these topologies is briefly described, and we discuss how they can be used to support electronic commerce.[16]

Table 6-2: Electronic commerce topologies

| **Topology** | Internet | Intranet | Interchain |
|---|---|---|---|
| Extent | Global | Organizational | Business partner-ship |
| Focus | Stakeholder relationships | Employee information and communication | Distribution channel communication |

The **Internet** is a global network of networks. Any computer connected to the Internet can communicate with any server in the system (see Figure 6-5). Thus, the Internet is well-suited to communicating with a wide variety of stakeholders. Adobe, for example, uses its Web site to distribute software changes to customers and provide financial and other reports to investors.

Many organizations have realized that Internet technology can also be used to establish an intra-organizational network that enables people within the organization to communicate and cooperate with each other. This so-called **Intranet** (see Figure 6-6) is essentially a fenced-off mini-Internet within an organization. A **firewall** (see page 141) is used to restrict access so that people outside the organization cannot access the Intranet. While an Intranet may

---

15. http://www.microsoft.com/jobs/
16. This section is based on Watson, R. T.; McKeown, P. G.; Garfield, M. Topologies for electronic cooperation. In: *Telecooperation in Organisations.* Lehner, F.; Dustdar, S., eds. Germany: Wiley-Teubner. 1997.

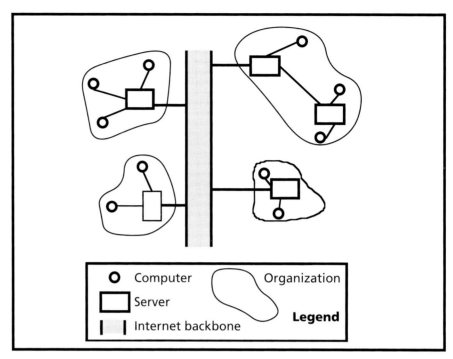

Figure 6-5. The Internet

not directly facilitate cooperation with external stakeholders, its ultimate goal
is to improve an organization's ability to serve these stakeholders.

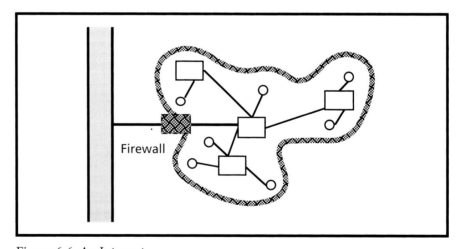

Figure 6-6. An Intranet

The Internet and Intranet, as the names imply, are networks. That is, an
array of computers can connect to each other. In some situations, however, an
organization may want to restrict connection capabilities so that instead of a
network there is a chain. An **Interchain** (see Figure 6-7) is designed to link a

buyer and supplier to facilitate greater coordination of common activities. The idea of an Interchain derives from the notion that each business has a **value chain**[17] and the end-point of one firm's chain links to the beginning of another's. Internet technology can be used to support communication and data transfer between two value chains. A chain, rather than a network, is established because communication is confined to the computers linking the two organizations. Of course, an organization could have multiple Interchains to link it with many other organizations, but each Interchain is specialized to support partnership coordination.

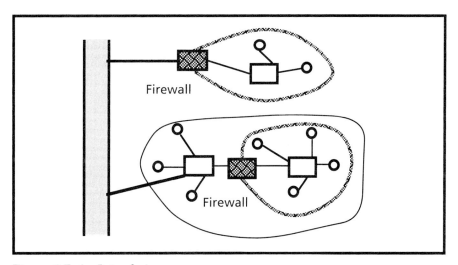

Figure 6-7. An Interchain

## The Inter-chain

The economies gained from low-cost Internet software and infrastructure means many more buyers and supplier pairs can now cooperate electronically. The cost of linking using Internet technology is an order of magnitude lower than using commercial communication networks for **electronic data interchange (EDI)**, the traditional approach for electronic cooperation between business partners.

EDI

EDI, which has been used for some 20 years, describes the electronic exchange of standard business documents between firms. A structured, standardized data format is used to exchange common business documents (e.g., invoices and shipping orders) between trading partners. In contrast to the free form of e-mail messages, EDI supports the exchange of repetitive, routine business transactions. Standards mean that routine electronic transactions can be concise and precise. The main standard used in the U.S. and Canada is known as ANSI X.12, and the United Nations has created an international standard called EDIFACT. Firms following the same standard can electroni-

---

17. For more on the value chain, see Porter, M. E. *Competitive advantage: creating and sustaining superior performance.* New York: Free Press, 1985.

cally share data. Before EDI, many standard messages between partners were generated by computer, printed, and mailed to the other party, who then manually entered the data into its computer. The main advantages of EDI are:

❖ paper handling is reduced, saving time and money;

❖ data are exchanged real time;

❖ there are fewer errors since data are only keyed once;

❖ enhanced data sharing enables greater coordination of activities between business partners;

❖ money flows are accelerated and payments received sooner.

Despite these advantages, for most companies EDI is still the exception, not the rule. A recent survey in the United States showed that almost 80 percent of the information flow between firms is on paper.   Paper should be the exception, not the rule. Most EDI traffic has been handled by **value-added networks (VANs)**[18] or private networks. However, these networks are too expensive for all but the largest 100,000 of the 6 million businesses in existence today in the United States. As a result, many businesses have not been able to participate in the benefits associated with EDI. However, the Internet may enable these smaller companies to take advantage of EDI.

Internet communication costs are significantly less than with traditional EDI. Accessing the Internet costs around $20 per month. These costs are probably at least half those of using a VAN. In addition, the Internet is a global network potentially accessible by nearly every firm. Consequently, there is every likelihood that the Internet will displace VANs as the electronic transport path between trading partners. Several VAN providers have announced plans to add the Internet to their menus of EDI service offerings. However, they warn they cannot give the same reliability and availability assurances about the Internet that they make for their own networks. Nevertheless, General Electric Information Services (GEIS) has launched an Internet-based electronic data interchange (EDI) service called GE TradeWeb.[19]

The simplest approach is to use the Internet as a means of replacing a VAN by using a commercially available Internet EDI package. EDI, with its roots in the 1960s, is a system for exchanging text, and the opportunity to use the multimedia capabilities of the Web is missed if a pure replacement strategy is applied. The multimedia capability of the Internet creates an opportunity for new applications that spawn a qualitatively different type of information exchange within a partnership. Once multimedia capability is added to the information exchange equation, then a new class of applications can be developed (e.g., educating the other partner in a firm's purchasing procedures). To reflect these new opportunities, we prefer to use the term Inter-

---

18. VANs add communication services to those provided by common carriers (e.g., AT&T in the U.S. and Telstra in Australia).

19. http://www.getradeweb.com/

chain rather than EDI. Manheim Auctions is an illustration of the opportunities offered by the Interchain.

An Interchain
case study

Manheim Auctions,[20] an Atlanta-based vehicle auction firm, with 50 plus auction sites in both the United States and Europe, auctions used vehicles to both retail dealers and to the general public. One particular type of vehicle that it handles is the so-called *program car*. This includes autos that have been used by auto company executives, coming off lease, or have been returned by automobile rental companies. When it receives a program car, the auto company typically turns these cars over to Manheim to dispose of at auctions around the country. In many situations, Manheim will receive a large number of program cars at a single location, which it then distributes around the country to avoid depressing the market for this type of automobile at the original receiving location. Moving these cars to other locations involves expenses that Manheim wants to avoid.

When a program car arrives at an auction site, dealer representatives from nearby cities and towns attend the auction to purchase vehicles that they believe are in demand in their locale. Occasionally, they will have an order from a buyer, but more often, they use their experience to choose cars. Once a car is purchased at auction, it is then driven or trucked to the dealer's lot for eventual retail sale. Using this process, the dealer has money tied up in inventory, plus the expense of sending a representative to the sale, and moving the automobile back to the lot. The dealer also is risking the cost of the vehicle in hope of eventually selling it.

Manheim decided that instead of using a real time auction, it would create a system to allow dealers to buy program cars at a set wholesale price determined by Manheim and the auto manufacturer. With this system, an authorized dealer with a personal computer connected to the Internet can purchase a program car by accessing the Manheim Web page, entering a user identifier and password, and then using a clickable query system to find a suitable auto to purchase. The Web page returned to the dealer contains information on vehicles that meet the specified needs. The page includes pictures of the vehicle and of any problems with it (dents, scratches, etc.). If the dealer decides to order this vehicle, Manheim will arrange transportation to the dealer's location.

Consider what the Manheim Interchain system allows the dealer to do. First, the dealer can wait until a customer has been identified before ordering the car from Manheim. In essence, the customer is ordering the program car through the dealer, and the dealer has far less risk in this transaction. Rather than sending a representative to an auction to purchase cars, which customers may or may not want, the dealer is able to order a car to a customer's specifications and have it delivered within a few days. Second, the dealer is not tying up funds in an inventory of cars awaiting a customer to purchase them. Instead, with the Manheim Interchain system, dealers have no money tied up in the transaction. They sell the car before they have to pay for it and, with

---

20. http://www.manheim.com/

Manheim's guarantee, they have no money at risk in the transaction. Finally, dealers do not bear the expense of employing and sending buyers to the program car auctions; instead, they simply query the Manheim database for cars that match customer needs. When first installed at a small number of dealers with only one auction site participating, the program was able to sell over $1 million in program cars in the first three weeks.

The Manheim case illustrates how a business partnership can cooperate electronically using an Interchain. We expect that because an Interchain lowers the costs of creating an inter-organizational system (IOS), many more business partnerships will move in this direction. Furthermore, an IOS is traditionally considered to support the flow of logistic (e.g., shipment status reports) and payment data (e.g., electronic funds transfers) between partners. Once multimedia capability is added to the information exchange equation, a new class of applications can be developed. An Interchain, for example, could be used to support the educational development of the other partner. Thus, we expect the notion of distribution channel coordination to broaden to support a wide range of a business partnership's activities.

## Security

**Security** is an eternal concern for organizations as they face the dual problem of protecting stored data and transported messages. Organizations have always had sensitive data to which they want to limit access to a few authorized people. Historically, such data have been stored in restricted areas (e.g., a vault) or encoded. These methods of restricting access and encoding are still appropriate.

Electronic commerce poses additional security problems. First, the intent of the Internet is to give people remote access to information. The system is inherently open, and traditional approaches of restricting access by the use of physical barriers are less viable, though organizations still need to restrict physical access to their servers. Second, because electronic commerce is based on computers and networks, these same technologies can be used to attack security systems. Hackers can use computers to intercept network traffic and scan it for confidential information. They can use computers to run repeated attacks on a system to breach its security (e.g., trying all words in the dictionary for an accounts password).

## Access control

**Data access control**, the major method of controlling access to stored data, often begins with some form of visitor authentication, though this is not always the case with the Web because many organizations are more interested in attracting rather than restricting visitors to their Web site. A variety of **authentication** mechanisms may be used (see Table 6-3). The common techniques for the Internet are account number, password, and IP address.

Table 6-3: Authentication mechanisms

| Class | Examples |
|---|---|
| Personal memory | Name, account number, password |
| Possessed object | Badge, plastic card, key, IP address |
| Personal characteristic | Fingerprint, voiceprint, signature, handsize |

**Using an Extranet to process mortgages**

At Countrywide Home Loans, the largest mortgage company in the United States, processing mortgage applications from one of its 500 partner banks used to take several days as information was faxed, telephoned, or mailed back and forth. However, today, a new Extranet system has reduced this time to less than one day. Countrywide's Extranet system is a hybrid Internet and Intranet system that enables the partner banks to use the Internet to gain access to Countrywide's Intranet.

When a partner bank is processing a loan application, it often needs information stored on Countrywide's Intranet. This includes loan status, account history, and interest rates. The Extranet system now allows a partner bank to point a Web browser at a secured Countrywide Web site, enter its name, password, ID number, and other secret proprietary information, and then access data pertinent to the loan. While there is a risk of exposing financial data to hackers or competitors, Countrywide has several layers of security, including Netscape's Secure Socket Layers (SSL) encryption methodology.

While not all of Countrywide's partner banks have signed up for the Extranet system, enough (200-300) have signed so that the mortgage company is experiencing "significant savings" in phone, paper, and mailing costs. The savings have been large enough to convince senior managers to approve a string of hybrid applications for the future.

Adapted from: Kim Nash, K. Extranet: best of both nets. *Computerworld*, August 12, 1996,: 1, 107.

Firewall

A system may often use multiple authentication methods to control data access, particularly because hackers are often persistent and ingenious in their efforts to gain unauthorized access. A second layer of defense can be a **firewall**, a device (e.g., a computer) placed between an organization's network and the Internet. This barrier monitors and controls all traffic between the Internet and the Intranet. Its purpose is to restrict the access of outsiders to the Intranet. A firewall is usually located at the point where the Intranet connects to the Internet, but it is also feasible to have firewalls within an Intranet to further restrict the access of those within the barrier.

There are several approaches to operating a firewall. The simplest method is to restrict traffic to packets with designated IP addresses (e.g., only permit those messages that come from the University of Georgia—i.e., the address ends with .uga.edu). Another screening rule is to restrict access to certain applications (e.g., Web pages). More elaborate screening rules can be implemented to decrease the ability of unauthorized people to access an Intranet.

Implementing and managing a firewall involves a tradeoff between the cost of maintaining the firewall and the loss caused by unauthorized access. An organization that simply wants to publicize its products and services may operate a simple firewall with limited screening rules. Alternatively, a firm that wants to share sensitive data with selected customers may install a more complex firewall to offer a high degree of protection.

## Coding

Coding or encryption techniques, as old as writing, have been used for thousands of years to maintain confidentiality. Although encryption is primarily used for protecting the integrity of messages, it can also be used to complement data access controls. There is always some chance that people will circumvent authentication controls and gain unauthorized access. To counteract this possibility, encryption can be used to obscure the meaning of data. The intruder cannot read the data without knowing the method of encryption and the key.

Societies have always needed secure methods of transmitting highly sensitive information and confirming the identity of the sender. In an earlier time, messages were sealed with the sender's personal signet ring—a simple, but easily forged, method of authentication. We still rely on personal signatures for checks and legal contracts, but how do you sign an e-mail message? In the information age, we need electronic encryption and signing for the orderly conduct of business, government, and personal correspondence.

Internet messages can pass through many computers on their way from sender to receiver, and there is always the danger that a **sniffer** program on an intermediate computer briefly intercepts and reads a message. In most cases, this will not cause you great concern, but what happens if your message contains your name, credit card number, and expiration date? The sniffer program, looking for a typical credit card number format of four blocks of four digits (e.g., 1234 5678 9012 3456), copies your message before letting it continue its normal progress. Now, the owner of the rogue program can use your credit card details to purchase products in your name and charge them to your account.

Without a secure means of transmitting payment information, customers and merchants will be very reluctant to place and receive orders, respectively. When the customer places an order, the Web browser should automatically encrypt the order prior to transmission—this is not the customer's task.

Credit card numbers are not the only sensitive information transmitted on the Internet. Because it is a general transport system for electronic information, the Internet can carry a wide range of confidential information (financial reports, sales figures, marketing strategies, technology reports, and so on). If senders and receivers cannot be sure that their communication is strictly private, they will not use the Internet. Secure transmission of information is necessary for electronic commerce to thrive.

Encryption

**Encryption** is the process of transforming messages or data to protect their meaning. Encryption scrambles a message so that it is meaningful only to the person knowing the method of encryption and the key to deciphering it. To everybody else, it is gobbledygook. The reverse process, **decryption**, converts a seemingly senseless character string into the original message. A popular form of encryption, readily available to Internet users, goes by the name of Pretty Good Privacy (PGP) and is distributed on the Web.[21] PGP is a public domain implementation of **public-key** encryption.

Traditional encryption, which uses the same key to encode and decode a message, has a very significant problem. How do you securely distribute the key? It can't be sent with the message because if the message is intercepted, the key can be used to decipher it. You must find another secure medium for transmitting the key. So, do you fax the key or phone it? Either method is not completely secure and is time consuming whenever the key is changed. Also, how do you know that the key's receiver will protect its secrecy?

A public-key encryption system has two keys: one private and the other public. A public key can be freely distributed because it is quite separate from its corresponding **private key**. To send and receive messages, communicators first need to create separate pairs of private and public keys and then exchange their public keys. The sender encrypts a message with the intended receiver's public key, and upon receiving the message, the receiver applies her private key (see Figure 6-8). The receiver's private key, the only one that can decrypt the message, must be kept secret to permit secure message exchange.

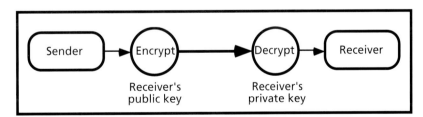

Figure 6-8. Encryption with a public-key system

The elegance of the public-key system is that it totally avoids the problem of secure transmission of keys. Public keys can be freely exchanged. Indeed, there can be a public database containing each person's or organization's

---

21. http://web.mit.edu/network/pgp

public key. For instance, if you want to e-mail your credit card details to a catalog company, you can simply obtain its public key (probably from its Web site) and encrypt your entire message prior to transmission. Of course, you may wish to transmit far more important data than your credit card number.

```
     To:    Pat McKeown <pmckeown@cbacc.cba.uga.edu>
   From:    Rick Watson <rwatson@uga.cc.uga.edu>
 Subject:   Money
-----------------------------------------------------------
G'day Pat
I hope you are enjoying your stay in Switzerland.

Could you do me a favor? I need $50,000 from my secret Swiss
bank account. The name of the bank is Aussie-Suisse Interna-
tional in Geneva. The account code is 451-3329 and the pass-
word is 'meekatharra'

I'll see you (and the money) at the airport this Friday.

Cheers

Rick
```

Figure 6-9. Message before encryption

Consider the message shown in Figure 6-9; the sender would hardly want this message to fall into the wrong hands. After encryption, the message is totally secure (see Figure 6-10). Only the receiver, using his private key, can decode the message.

```
     To:    Pat McKeown <pmckeown@cbacc.cba.uga.edu>
   From:    Rick Watson <rwatson@uga.cc.uga.edu>
 Subject:   Money
-----------------------------------------------------------
-----BEGIN PGP MESSAGE-----
Version: 2.6.2

hEwDfOTG8eEvuiEBAf9rxBdHpgdq1g0gaIP7zm1OcHvWHtx+9++ip27q6vI
tjYbIUKDnGjV0sm2INWpcohrarI9S2xU6UcSPyFfumGs9pgAAAQ0euRGjZY
RgIPE5DUHG uItXYsnIq7zFHVevjO2dAEJ8ouaIX9YJD8kwp4T3suQnw7/d
1j4ed146qisrQHpRRwqHXons7w4k04x8tH4JGfWEXc5LB+hcOSyPHEir4EP
qDcEPlblM9bH6 w2ku2fUmdMaoptnVSinLMtzSqIKQlHMfaJ0HM9Df4kWh+
ZbY0yFXxSuHKrgbaoDcu9wUze35dtwiCTdf1sf3ndQNaLOFiIjh5pis+bUg
9rOZjxpEFbdGgYpcfBB4rvRNwOwizvSodxJ9H+VdtAL3DIsSJdNSAEuxjQ0
hvOSA8oCBDJfHSUFqX3ROtB3+yuT1vf/C8Vod4gW4tvqj8C1QNte+ehxg==
=fD44
-----END PGP MESSAGE-----
```

Figure 6-10. Message after encryption

Signing

In addition, a public-key encryption system can be used to authenticate messages. In cases where the content of the message is not confidential, the receiver may still wish to verify the sender's identity. For example, one of your friends may find it amusing to have some fun at your expense (see Figure 6-11).

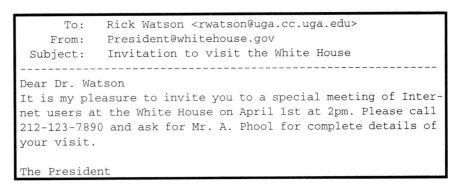

```
       To:    Rick Watson <rwatson@uga.cc.uga.edu>
      From:   President@whitehouse.gov
   Subject:   Invitation to visit the White House
-------------------------------------------------------------
Dear Dr. Watson
It is my pleasure to invite you to a special meeting of Inter-
net users at the White House on April 1st at 2pm. Please call
212-123-7890 and ask for Mr. A. Phool for complete details of
your visit.

The President
```

Figure 6-11. Message before signing

If the President indeed was in the habit of communicating electronically, it is likely that he would sign his messages so that the receiver could verify it. A sender's private key is used to created **a signed message**. The receiver then applies the sender's public key to verify the signature (see Figure 6-12).

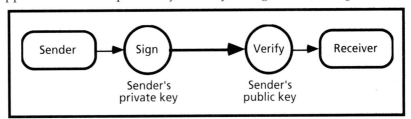

Figure 6-12. Signing with a public-key system

A signed message has additional encrypted text containing the sender's signature (see Figure 6-13). When the purported sender's public key is applied to this message, the identity of the sender can be verified (it was not the President).

Imagine you pay $1,000 per year for an investment information service. The provider might want to verify that any e-mail requests it receives are from subscribers. Thus, as part of the subscription sign-up, subscribers have to supply their public key, and when using the service, sign all electronic messages with their private key. The provider is then assured that it is servicing paying customers. Naturally, any messages between the service and the client should be encrypted to ensure that others do not gain from the information.

```
            To:    Rick Watson <rwatson@uga.cc.uga.edu>
          From:    President@whitehouse.gov
       Subject:    Invitation to visit the White House
-------------------------------------------------------------
Dear Dr. Watson
It is my pleasure to invite you to a special meeting of Inter-
net users at the White House on April 1st at 2pm. Please call
212-123-7890 and ask for Mr. A. Phool for complete details of
your visit.

The President
-----BEGIN PGP SIGNATURE-----
Version: 2.6.2
iQCVAwUBMeRVVUblZxMqZR69AQFJNQQAwHMSrZhWyiGTieGukbhPGUNF3aB
+qm7E8g5ySsY6QqUcg2zwUr40w8Q0Lfcc4nmr0NUujiXkqzTNb+3RL41w5x
fTCfMp1Fi5Hawo829UQAlmN8L5hzl7XfeON5WxfYcxLGXZcbUWkGio6/d4r
9Ez6s79DDf9EuDlZ4qfQcy1iA==G6jB
-----END PGP SIGNATURE-----
```

Figure 6-13. Message after signing

## Electronic money

When commerce goes electronic, the means of paying for goods and services must also go electronic. Paper-based payment systems cannot support the speed, security, privacy, and internationalization necessary for electronic commerce. In this section, we discuss four methods of electronic payment:

❖ electronic funds transfer

❖ digital cash

❖ ecash

❖ credit card

There are four fundamental concerns regarding electronic money: security, **authentication, anonymity,** and **divisibility**. Consumers and organizations need to be assured that their on-line orders are protected and organizations must be able to transfer securely large millions of dollars. Buyers and sellers must be able to verify that the electronic money they receive is real; consumers must have faith in electronic currency. Transactions, when required, should remain confidential. Electronic currency must be spendable in small amounts (e.g., less than one-tenth of a cent) so that high-volume, small-value Internet transactions are feasible (e.g., paying 0.1 cent to read an article in an encyclopedia). The various approaches to electronic money vary in their capability to solve these concerns (see Table 6-4).

Any money system, real or electronic, must have a reasonable level of security and a high level of authentication, otherwise people will not use it. All electronic money systems are potentially divisible. There is a need, however, to adapt some systems so that transactions can be automated. For example, you do not want to have to type your full credit card details each time you spend .01 cent. A modified credit card system, which automatically sent previously stored details from your personal computer, could be used for small transactions.

Table 6-4: Characteristics of electronic money

|  | Security | Authentication | Anonymity | Divisibility |
|---|---|---|---|---|
| EFT | High | High | Low | Yes |
| Digital cash | Medium | High | High | Yes |
| Ecash | High | High | High | Yes |
| Credit card | High | High | Low | Yes |

The technical problems of electronic money have not been completely solved, but many people are working on their solution because electronic money promises efficiencies that will reduce the costs of transactions between buyers and sellers. It will also enable access to the global marketplace. In the next few years, electronic currency will displace notes and coins for many transactions.

## Electronic funds transfer

**Electronic funds transfer** (EFT), introduced in the late 1960s, uses the existing banking structure to support a wide variety of payments. For example, consumers can establish monthly checking account deductions for utility bills, and banks can transfer millions of dollars. EFT is essentially electronic checking. Instead of writing a check and mailing it, the buyer initiates an electronic checking transaction (e.g., using a debit card at a point-of-sale terminal). The transaction is then electronically transmitted to an intermediary (usually the banking system), which transfers the funds from the buyer's account to the seller's account. A banking system has one or more common clearinghouses that facilitate the flow of funds between accounts in different banks.

Electronic checking is fast; transactions are instantaneous. Paper handling costs are substantially reduced. Bad checks are no longer a problem because the seller's account balance is verified at the moment of the transaction. EFT is flexible; it can handle high volumes of consumer and commercial transactions, both locally and internationally. The international payment clearing system, consisting of more than 100 financial institutions, handles an average of $1.2 trillion per day.

The major shortfall of EFT is that all transactions must pass through the banking system, which is legally required to record every transaction. This lack of privacy can have serious consequences.[22] Cash gives anonymity.

## Digital cash

**Digital cash** is an electronic parallel of notes and coins. Two variants of digital cash are presently available: prepaid cards and smart cards. The phonecard, the most common form of prepaid card, was first issued in 1976 by the

---

22. A defrocked Buddhist monk left a credit card transaction trail when he visited an Australian brothel. (Police asked to examine credit card pay slips. *Bangkok Post.* Feb. 24 1995; 50(55):1)

forerunner of Telecom Italia.[23] The problem with special-purpose cards, such as phone and photocopy cards, is that people end up with a purse or wallet full of cards. A **smart card** combines many functions into one card. A smart card can serve as personal identification, credit card, ATM card, telephone credit card, critical medical information record and as *cash* for small transactions. A smart card, containing memory and a microprocessor, can store as much as 100 times more data than a magnetic-stripe card. The microprocessor can be programmed.

The stored-value card, the most common application of smart card technology, can be used to purchase a wide variety of items (e.g,. fast food, parking, public transport tickets). Consumers buy cards of standard denominations (e.g., $20, $50, or $100) from a card dispenser or bank. When the card is used to pay for an item, it must be inserted in a reader. Then the amount of the transaction is transferred to the reader, and the value of the card is reduced by the transaction amount.

The problem with digital cash, like real cash, is that you can lose it or it can be stolen. It is not as secure as the other alternatives, but most people are likely to carry only small amounts of digital cash and thus security is not so critical. As smart cards are likely to have a unique serial number, consumers can limit their loss by reporting a stolen or misplaced smart card to invalidate its use. Adding a PIN number to a smart card can raise its security level.

Twenty million smart cards are already in use in France, where they were introduced a decade earlier. In Austria, 2.5 million consumers already carry a card that has an ATM magnetic stripe as well as a smart card chip. Stored-value cards are likely to be in widespread use in the United States within five years. Their wide-scale adoption could provide substantial benefits. Counting, moving, storing and safeguarding cash is estimated to be 4 percent of the value of all transactions. There are also significant benefits to be gained because banks, having to hold less cash on hand, will have more money available for investment.

## Ecash

Digicash[24] of Amsterdam has developed an electronic payment system called **ecash** that can be used to withdraw and deposit electronic cash over the Internet. The system is designed to provide secure payment between computers using e-mail or the Internet. Ecash can be used for everyday Internet transactions, such as buying software, receiving money from parents, or paying for a pizza to be delivered. At the same time, ecash provides the privacy of cash because the payer can remain anonymous.

To use ecash you need a digital bank account (the Mark Twain Bank of Missouri opened for business in October 1995) and ecash client software. The client is used to withdraw ecash from your bank account, and store it on your personal computer. You can then spend the money at any location accepting ecash or send money to someone who has an ecash account.

---

23. See this card at http://www.agora.stm.it/L.Costa/firstph.htm

24. http://www.digicash.com/

The security system is based on public-key cryptography (See "Security" on page 140) and passwords. You need a password to access your account and electronic transactions are encrypted.

---

**Cash cards go to the Olympics—but no gold**

Visa set up 4,200 terminals at 1,500 merchants in Atlanta to serve Olympic visitors using cash cards, which could be purchased at dispensers and banks within Atlanta. The cards could be used at Hartsfield International Airport, inside the Olympic Ring, Olympic venues, and MARTA rail stations. In the first ten days of the Olympics, there were 269,000 transactions totaling $951,000. Nearly 50 percent of Atlanta consumers were aware of the cards, but only 5 percent had used them. Consumer awareness was created, but acceptance was lagging, particularly as street vendors and ticket scalpers didn't take cash cards.

Adapted from: Bond, P. Cash cards off to a slow start. *Atlanta Journal-Constitution.*; Aug. 2, 1996; D: 1.

---

*Credit card*

**Credit cards** are a safe, secure, and widely used remote payment system. Millions of people use them everyday for ordering goods by phone. Furthermore, people think nothing of handing over their card to a restaurant server, who could easily find time to write down the card's details. In the case of fraud, banks already protect consumers, who are typically liable for only the first $50. So, why worry about sending your credit card number over the Internet? The development of secure servers and clients will make transmitting credit card numbers extremely safe. Visa and Microsoft have a joint project to develop software to make on-line purchases using coded credit card numbers. The major shortcomings of credit cards is that they do not support person-to-person transfers and do not have the privacy of cash.

## Conclusion

Electronic commerce is a new way of doing business. Internet technology has created a business revolution because it changes the form and extent of communication between an organization and its stakeholders, especially customers. Organizations must master this new technology and understand the opportunities and threats it presents. More importantly, they must comprehend how technological change will revolutionize their business. The Internet, and the Web in particular, offers many opportunities for organizations to redesign their present business practices to reduce demand, innovation, and inefficiency risk. Businesses must analyze and exploit these opportunities if they are to make the transition to an information economy.

## Key terms and concepts

anonymity
authentication
business service
communication flip-flop
credit card
customer convergence
data access control
data transport
decryption
demand risk
digital cash
divisibility
ecash
electronic commerce application
electronic commerce topology
electronic data interchange (EDI)
electronic funds transfer (EFT)
electronic publishing
encryption
firewall

inefficiency risk
information intensity
innovation risk
Intranet
Interchain
Internet
message distribution
national information infrastructure
private key
public key
security
signed message
smart card
sniffer
stakeholder
transmission control protocol/
    Internet protocol (TCP/IP)
value-added network (VAN)
value chain

## Exercises

1. Choose three businesses with which you are familiar. Of the three strategic challenges, which do you think is the most threatening to each of these businesses? How might they use the Web to reduce the risks?

2. What is the communications flip-flop?

3. Identify two or three organizations that fit into each quadrant of the Web presence grid, and visit their home pages. What do you observe?

4. Prepare a report on how an organization is using the Intranet.

5. Find some examples of the Interchain, and describe the benefits to the business partnership.

6. What's the difference between encrypting and signing?

7. Retrieve a copy of PGP and generate a pair of keys.

8. What are the advantages of ecash?

9. Investigate how Visa is developing technology to support use of its credit card for electronic commerce.

10. How could universities or colleges take advantage of smart card technology?

# 7      Managing electronic commerce

■ ■ ■ ■ ■ ■ ■ ■ ■ ■ ■ ■ ■ ■ ■ ■ ■ ■ ■ ■ ■ ■ ■ ■ ■ ■ ■ ■ ■ ■ ■ ■ ■ ■ ■ ■

**Objectives**

After completing this chapter, you will be able to:

❖ apply the principles of designing an electronic commerce strategy for an organization;

❖ use the customer service life cycle and Integrated Internet Marketing models to identify opportunities for organizations to use electronic commerce;

❖ measure the efficiency of a Web site.

**Introduction**

This chapter presents some useful frameworks and examples for stimulating thinking about an organization's management and development of electronic commerce. The first requirement is for a systematic approach to developing a strategy. Once a strategy has been developed, there is a need for some frameworks to assist in identifying possible applications. Frameworks provide a structure to aid systematic consideration of opportunities. Once a Web site has been developed, managers need ways of measuring its efficiency. This chapter is supported by a wide variety of Web sites that demonstrate the principles discussed. Examples foster analogical thinking—"We have a situation similar to that example. With a few modifications and twists, we could do the same."

**Strategy**

A Web site that attracts very few visitors or the wrong type of visitors is a very poor investment. Thus, organizations need to consider whom they want to attract to their Web site and how they might attract them. Organizations want to create Web sites that many people visit. The Web site is an **attractor**. As a rule, an organization should concentrate on attracting the most influential stakeholders. Remember, these are the groups that can determine an enterprise's future. Usually, an organization will want to attract prospective customers, but there are other groups that can impact the future of the organization and can be the target of a Web site. For example, a firm might use its Web site to communicate with employees, or it may want to attract and inform investors and potential suppliers. Once the targeted **stakeholder** group has been selected, the organization needs to decide the degree of personalization of its interaction with this group.

We put forward a two-stage process for identifying the strategic properties of a Web site (see Figure 7-1). First, identify the stakeholder group to be influenced by making the site more attractive to this group—the **influence filter**. Second, decide the degree of customization—the **target refractor**.

The Kellogg's Company,[1] for instance, lets young visitors pick a drawing and color it by selecting from a palette and clicking on segments of the picture. This Web site, designed to appeal to all young children, filters but is not customized. All children get the same portfolio of drawings to color.

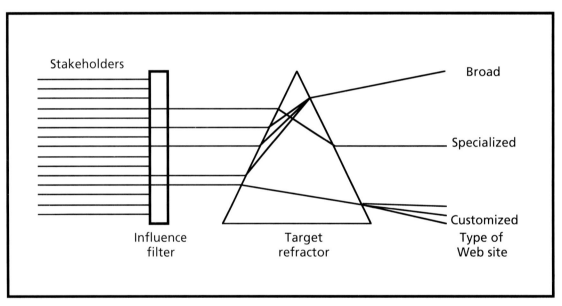

Figure 7-1. Web strategies

Information technology permits a Web site to be individually tailored to each visitor. That is, different visitors may see a different page layout or set of pages. For instance, Kellogg's could change its Web site according to the home country of the visitor[2] (e.g., Australian children see pictures of kangaroos and koala bears and South African kids can color lions and elephants).

---

1. http://www.kelloggs.com/
2. This can be determined from the rightmost portion of an address.

Therefore, the second stage of strategic planning is to decide the degree of customization of a Web site: broad, specialized, or customized.

**Broad.** A Web site can communicate with a number of types of stakeholders or many of the people in one stakeholder category. For example, Goodyear Tire & Rubber Company's Web site,[3] with its information on tires, is directed at the general tire customer. A broad Web site provides content with minimal adjustment to the needs of the visitor. Thus, many visitors may not linger too long at the site because there is little that particularly catches their attention.

**Specialized.** A specialized attractor appeals to a more narrow audience. Federal Express,[4] for instance, with its parcel tracking system has decided to focus on current customers. A customer can enter a receipt number to determine the current location of a package and download software for preparing transportation documentation. A specialized Web site may attract fewer visitors, but nearly all those who make the link find the visit worthwhile.

**Customized.** The marketer's dream is to develop an interactive relationship with individual customers. Database technology and back-end application software enable a Web site to be customized to meet the needs of the individual. Computer magazine publisher Ziff-Davis[5] offers visitors the opportunity to specify a personal profile. After completing a registration form, the visitor can then select what to see on future visits. For instance, a marketing manager tracking the CAD/CAM software market in Germany can set a profile that displays links to new stories on these topics. On future visits to the Ziff-Davis site, the manager can click on the personal view button to access the latest news matching the profile. The Mayo Clinic[6] uses the Internet chat facility to host a series of monthly on-line forums with Clinic specialists. The forums are free, and questions may be asked directly of an endocrinologist, for instance. Thus, visitors can get advice on their particular ailments.

There are two types of personalized attractors. **Adaptable sites** can be customized by the visitor, as in the case of Ziff-Davis. The visitor establishes what is of interest by answering questions or selecting options. An **adaptive site** learns from the visitor's behavior and determines what should be presented. Firefly[7] is an early instance of a learning, adaptive Web site. It tries to discover what type of music the visitor likes so that it can recommend CDs.

We foresee the emergence of Web applications that use the visitor's previously gathered demographic data and record of pages browsed to create dynamically a tailored set of Web pages, just as magazines can be personalized.

3. http://www.goodyear.com/Home/HTML/Educational/TireSchool/TireSchool.html
4. http://www.fedex.com/
5. http://www.zdnet.com
6. http://www.mayo.ivi.com/
7. http://www.ffly.com/

**━ ━━ ━ ━━ ━ ━ ━ ━ ━ ━━ ━ ━━ ━ ━ ━ ━ ━ ━ ━ ━ ━ ━ ━**

# Your turn!

1. Select an organization (e.g., your employer or college) and identify the stakeholders it might want to attract to its Web site.

2. For three of the stakeholders identified in the preceding step, decide on the degree of specialization of the Web site.

3. Using Firefly as an example, identify some other organizations that are candidates for an adaptive Web site.

**━ ━ ━━ ━ ━ ━━ ━ ━ ━ ━ ━ ━ ━ ━ ━ ━ ━ ━ ━ ━ ━ ━ ━ ━**

## Identifying applications

Upon completion of the strategic design of a Web site, the next step is to identify applications that will attract stakeholders to visit. Managers frequently find it more useful to have models to focus their thinking and examples to stimulate creativity. In this section, two models are presented: the customer service life cycle and Integrated Internet Marketing. Each component of these models is accompanied by an illustrative case. The combination of a business model and an example should kindle generation of thoughts for Web use.

### Customer service life cycle

The **customer service life cycle**[8] separates the service relationship with a customer into four major phases (see Figure 7-2), which are:

❖ **Requirements**: assisting the customer to determine needs (e.g., photographs of a product, video presentations, textual descriptions, articles or reviews, sound bytes of a CD, and downloadable demonstration files);

❖ **Acquisition**: helping the customer to acquire a product or service (e.g., on-line order entry, downloadable software);

❖ **Ownership**: supporting the customer on an ongoing basis (e.g., interactive on-line user groups, on-line technical support, frequently asked questions, resource libraries, newsletters, on-line renewal of subscriptions);

❖ **Retirement**: helping the client to dispose of the service or product (e.g., on-line resale, classified ads).

Examples for each major phase demonstrate how some organizations are currently using the Web.

---

8. Ives, B.; Learmonth, G. P. The information systems as a competitive weapon. *Communications of the ACM.* 1984, 27 (12): 1193-1201.

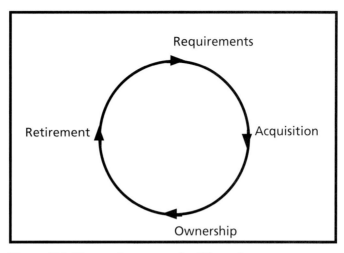

Figure 7-2. The customer service life cycle

Requirements          Hotel chain Promus[9] helps customers determine which of its three chains matches their travel plans. As an example, for its Embassy Suites, it shows a photo of a typical room and hotel. A complete directory of hotels, with telephone numbers for reservations, is provided for more than 30 countries. The information provided for each hotel includes: locale data; directions to the hotel; a description of the hotel and nearby attractions, restaurants, businesses, and cities; and a complete list of the hotel's facilities. Compared to a paper directory, the Web is far easier to use and contains considerably more detail.

Selecting computer hardware is a difficult task because there are many manufacturers offering a wide range of configurations. Hewlett Packard[10] provides complete details of its various products, including major features, specification of the hardware, and available options (see Figure 7-3).

Once you have made your fortune on the Web, you may want to indulge in the ultimate in automotive conspicuous consumption—a Rolls-Royce. To help you decide your requirements—the Corniche IV or Silver Spirit III— check out EuroMotors in Washington.[11] You can see photos of the interior and exterior and review the technical details. The list price would be quite useful, but then if you have to ask, you probably cannot afford a Rolls-Royce.

Using the Web for requirements information reduces the time and cost of delivering information to customers. Furthermore, a well-designed Web site can accelerate information retrieval by helping the customer navigate to needed information. Organizations can go even further; an expert system could be used to ensure customers find the most relevant information. For example, Dell could use a series of questions (e.g., Will you use the system for desktop publishing?) to quickly narrow the range of feasible computers.

9. http://www.promus.com/

10. http://www.hp.com/

11. http://www.euromotorcars.com/rolls.htm

Figure 7-3.  Product summary of a Hewlett Packard scanner

Acquisition

Many customers know how to buy flowers via the telephone—you simply dial 1-800-FLOWERS or the toll-free number of any florist. However, when you order by phone, you may find it hard to visualize the floral arrangement because you must rely on the order taker's verbal description. And remember the time the recipient's name was misunderstood—it certainly deflated the impact of the flowers. Web ordering solves both of these problems. You can see photos of the floral arrangements and enter the message to accompany the flowers. Once you provide credit card information, the order is complete. Many florists (e.g., Lane and Lenge[12]) now take orders over the Web.

Just about any item can be sold on the Web. For example, if you are concerned about the proportion of lead in the paint of an old house, you can order a $12.95 lead testing kit.[13] In addition to the order form, the page gives facts about lead and describes how to use the testing kit. The Web offers the opportunity for a small business, maybe with a single product, to reach an international market.

Web ordering has two major advantages. First, the customer enters the data into the computer, thus reducing the need for employees to do this task. Second, the firm has less need to synchronize its activities with its customers. For instance, a firm that receives many phone orders during the evening will

12. http://www.flower.net/

13. http://branch.com:80/epa/

## Going on-line for better service

Have you ever called the service department of a company to find out why their product is not working as advertised and, after going through a long list of voice mail menus, found yourself put on seemingly interminable hold, forced to listen to repeated messages extolling the virtues of the product you can't make work? If so, then you are a candidate for a growing use of the Internet: on-line customer service. Pioneered by computer hardware and software companies with their bulletin board services, customer service is now available over the Internet through a variety of FTP archives, Newsgroups, mailing lists, Gopher sites, and, of course, the Web. For example, by clicking on Support at the Microsoft Web site, you can obtain help on a variety of problems ranging from formatting in Word to troubleshooting CD-ROM products for children. There is also a list of frequently asked questions (FAQs), a knowledge base that can be searched, and a location from which you can download a fix for a problem with a Microsoft product. Other hardware and software companies have similar Web sites.

However, today, on-line service is not restricted to the computer companies. For example, Gatorade has a Web page that provides much information about the sports drink as well as the capability to send comments to Gatorade about the product. These comments are often answered by a group of customer service representatives. A support site for the increasing number of women who are surfing the Net is the Clinique Web site. This site includes information on all of Clinique's beauty products as well as a skin-analysis program to help customers decide on the best Clinique product for them. There is also a library of beauty tips and advice from visiting experts. There is even a section *Just for Men* as well as a women's guide to the Web.

Many believe that companies have just scratched the surface of on-line customer support with their current Web sites. New technologies including streaming audio and video and virtual reality may soon make it possible for customers to ask questions and receive answers on a real-time basis from virtual service representatives. Software in the form of intelligent agents may also recognize repeat customers and instantly suggest solutions in the form of expert advice or upgrades.

Adapted from: Resnick, R. Service with a modem. *Internet World*, September 1996: 38-40.

have to employ sufficient staff during that period to handle peak traffic. As a result, if it is particularly concerned with customer service, it may well be overstaffed for much of the period because it is carrying slack to handle the peak load. While orders received via the Web should be handled expeditiously, the firm has better control over the scheduling of its employees because it breaks the nexus between the customer and the order taker.

Ownership    Every household in America is served by the U.S. Postal Service (USPS).[14] In terms of the customer service life cycle, each household owns a postal service that delivers mail to its address. USPS can make this service more efficient if every customer uses the full nine-digit ZIP code for addressing mail. Its Web site, as well as including details of current postal charges, has an interactive form that permits retrieval of the full ZIP for any U.S. address (see Figure 7-4). Simply complete the form, click on the Submit button (not shown in Figure 7-4), and within a few seconds the full ZIP is displayed. Imagine the cost savings if every consumer used this service.

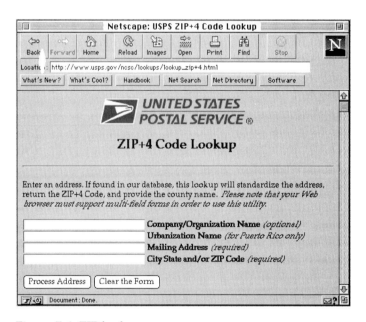

Figure 7-4. ZIP lookup

Citibank operates a worldwide banking business and has branches in many parts of the world. Customers can find their nearest branch by using Citibank's branch locator. This is handy for travelers or someone who has just moved into a new neighborhood. In addition, Citibank provides details of the full range of services available to its customers (e.g., mortgages, credit cards, and money management accounts).

14. http://www.usps.gov/

Many businesses and consumers use UPS[15] to deliver parcels. To find the nearest of nearly 50,000 UPS drop-off addresses, customers can use the UPS drop-off locator. There is also a calculator for estimating the cost of sending a package, and customers can use the Web for requesting pickup of an item. If you know an item's tracking number, you can find its current status by completing a form on the UPS Web site.

The three preceding examples demonstrate how organizations are using the Web during the ownership phase of the customer service life cycle. Notice that in each case, the organization is improving customer service and lowering its costs. The U.S. Postal Service will save on mail processing if more people use the full ZIP. Citibank can reduce the number of glossy brochures of check designs it mails to customers. It could even go one step further and interactively show customers how the check will look once their preferences are given. UPS can reduce the number of service personnel required to answer phone queries.

Retirement    Most of the organizations using the Web for the retirement phase of the customer service life cycle are in recycling. The Global Recycling Network (GRN)[16] is an electronic market to help businesses find possible trading partners for the sale of recyclable goods—raw materials, industrial by-products, used or rebuilt equipment, or unwanted machinery. Subscribers to GRN's on-line database add new trade opportunities every day. Businesses connected to GRN can make real-time buy and sell offers. Because GRN is on the Web, the service is international and can link companies anywhere.

Power Express,[17] which sells batteries, provides details of how to recycle used batteries. Advice on how to recycle or reuse laser and ink-jet cartridges is supplied by Ribbon-Jet Trek.[18]

The Web seems to be particularly well-suited to support recycling because the market for used goods is rarely well-organized. The problem is that it is often difficult for buyers and sellers to find each other. Most markets for used products are local (e.g., the classified advertisements in the local newspaper). Going global with the Web greatly expands the size of the market and increases the potential of buyers and sellers finding each other. This is true for many markets that are difficult to sustain regionally.

■ ■ ■ ■ ■ ■ ■ ■ ■ ■ ■ ■ ■ ■ ■ ■ ■ ■ ■ ■ ■

## Your turn!

1. Visit the Promus site and select a hotel for your next vacation.

2. Use the USPS Web page to determine the full ZIP of John Wiley & Sons' New York office.

---

15. http://www.ups.com
16. http://grn.com/grn/
17. http://www.powerexpress.com/battbible.html
18. http://www.rmi.net/rjtek/

3.  Take each phase of the customer service life cycle (e.g., requirements) and find Web sites that illustrate support for this phase. Send your answer to Rick Watson (rwatson@uga.cc.uga.edu) so he can add this information to this book's Web site.[19]

■ ■ ■ ■ ■ ■ ■ ■ ■ ■ ■ ■ ■ ■ ■ ■ ■ ■ ■ ■ ■ ■ ■ ■ ■ ■ ■

*Integrated Internet Marketing (I²M)*

The interactive and multimedia capabilities of the Web, combined with other Internet facilities such as e-mail's support for personal and mass communication, present a range of tools for interacting with customers. Furthermore, the Web can provide easy-to-use, front-end to back-end applications using, for example, databases[20] and expert systems technology. Consequently, the Internet offers an excellent basis for a variety of marketing tactics, and we can develop a model for **Integrated Internet Marketing** (I²M).[21] [22]I²M (see Figure 7-5) is the coordination of Internet facilities to market products and services, shape stakeholders' (customers in particular) attitudes, and establish or maintain a corporate image. The central idea of I²M is that an organization should coordinate its use of the Internet to develop a coherent, synchronous marketing strategy. The following examples demonstrate how some organizations use particular features of the Web for elements of the I²M model.

News stories

Traditionally, organizations have relied on news media and advertisements to transmit their stories to the customer. The use of intermediaries, however, can pose problems. For example, news stories, not reported as envisaged, can result in the customer receiving a distorted, unintended message. When dealing with the Pentium hullabaloo, Intel's CEO Groves used the Internet to communicate directly with customers.

---

19. http://www.negia.net/webbook

20. For example, see the MIS faculty directory, which is stored on an SQL database and accessed via the Web (http://webfoot.csom.umn.edu/isworld/facdir/home.htm).

21. Portions of this section are adapted from Zinkhan, G. M.; Watson, R. T. Advertising trends: innovation and the process of creative destruction. *Journal of Business Research.* 1996; 37, 163-171.

22. Some of these ideas are based on Schultz, D. E.; Tannenbaum, S. I.; Lauterborn, R. F. *The new marketing paradigm: integrated marketing communications.* Lincolnwood, IL: NTC Business Books, 1994.

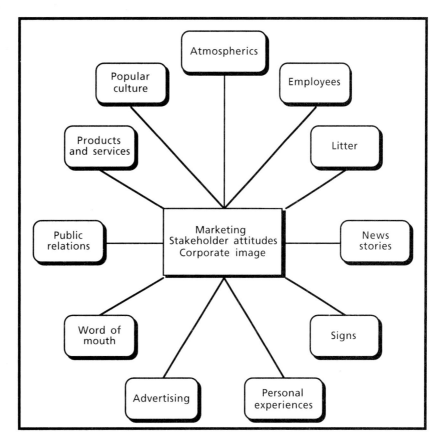

Figure 7-5. Components and processes that influence corporate image and customer attitudes

Advertising    The hyperlink, a key feature of the Web, permits a reader to jump to another Web site by clicking on a link. An advertiser can place hyperlink signs or logos at relevant points on the Web so that interested readers may be enticed to link to the advertiser's Web site. For example, Prentice-Hall pays ISWorld Net[23] to display its logo prominently on ISWorld Net's home page, which provides an entry point to Web resources for IS academics and professionals. As a publisher of information systems textbooks, Prentice-Hall anticipates that potential adopters will follow the link to the Web site, where they can find details of relevant books, including sample chapters and support materials.

Hyperlinks are the billboards of the information highway. They are most valuable when they appear on Web pages read by potential consumers. As it is very easy to record the number of links from one page to another, it will be simple for advertisers to place a value on a particular hyperlink and for the owners of these pages to demand an appropriate rent.

---

23. http://www.isworld.org/isworld.html

Atmospherics    Many organizations are interested in the ambiance or *atmospherics* their establishment creates for the customer. The Web provides an opportunity for customers to experience an organization's atmospherics without actually being there. For example, Alberto's Nightclub (introduced in Chapter 1) in Mountain View, California[24] stimulates interest by creating an aura of excitement and action. The visual on its home page exudes the ethos of the club (Figure 7-6). An accompanying photo of the nightclub shows a crowded dance floor of young people.

Figure 7-6. Alberto's Nightclub

If customers are reluctant to visit Alberto's because they can't dance the salsa, then they can step into the virtual ballroom where the dance step is displayed. Voice instructions, for male or female steps, are available to help with the timing of the dance's steps. Instructions are available for 11 other dances. If personal lessons are desired, the customer can see a photo of the attractive instructors. Alberto's also provides a map for finding the nightclub.

Alberto's can go further by adding a video clip of the dance floor crowd and including some dance music. These additions would enhance the on-line atmosphere of a night at Alberto's.

Employees    E-mail and lists have become effective methods of communicating with employees, particularly for highly dispersed international organizations. Problems can be swiftly pushed up the hierarchy and decisions distributed quickly throughout the organization. As a result, a marketing problem in Hong Kong can be solved by an executive in Germany, and within minutes, the solution can be distributed to all relevant employees. Effective use of electronic communication permits rapid problem detection. Because policy

---

24. http://albertos.com/albertos/

changes can be distributed inexpensively and instantly, the organization can gain a high degree of consistency in its communications with employees and other stakeholders.

Also, an organization can develop a Web application focusing on employee communication. Instead of an in-house newsletter, the Web can be used to keep employees informed of company developments. The advantage is that previous issues of the newsletter can be made available, perhaps via a search engine, and there can be links to other related articles. For example, a story on new health benefits can have links to the firm's benefits policy manual.

Use of e-mail and the Web should lead to consistent internal communication, a necessary prerequisite of consistent external communication with customers, suppliers, shareholders, and other parties. A well-informed employee is likely to feel greater involvement with the organization and more able to perform effectively.

Litter

The discarded Big Mac wrapper blowing across the highway does little for MacDonald's corporate image. On the Internet, an advertisement arriving along with other e-mail may be perceived by some readers as highly offensive electronic pollution. An Arizona lawyer who posted an advertisement to millions of Internet users aroused considerable ire. The avalanche of e-mail complaints to him crashed his Internet service supplier's computer 15 times. The reaction spawned a program, based in Finland, that seeks out mass postings and deletes them. Of course, this raises the issue of who has the right to decide what advertising, or any other message for that matter, should be censored. Also, do some countries become havens for electronic terrorists whose programs wander the Internet, destroying what they consider improper or inappropriate?

Signs

Most organizations prominently display their logos and other identifying signs on their buildings, packaging, and other visual points of customer contact. There has been a clear transfer of this concept to the Web. A corporate logo frequently is visually reinforced by placing it on each Web page.

Organizations can be extremely creative in their use of signs. Reykjavik Advertising,[25] with a collection of pages for a variety of Icelandic clients, makes clever use of the puffin, Iceland's national bird. Reykjavik Advertising's so-called traffic puffin indicates movement relative to a page hierarchy—back, up, or forward, respectively (see Figure 7-7). It is an interesting alternative to the bland arrows of a Web browser. The traffic puffin appears on each page. After viewing the pages, a clear impression of the resourceful use of the puffin remains. A new medium creates opportunities for reinventing signs.

Animation is another way firms can reinvent their signs. Manheim Auctions,[26] the Atlanta-headquartered car auction firm, uses animation to reinforce recognition of its corporate logo. The inner part of its circular logo

25. http://www.arctic.is/ad/ad.html
26. http://www.manheim.com/

Figure 7-7. Innovative use of a sign

rotates. Animation catches the eye and makes the visitor more aware of the Manheim logo.

Personal experience

Customers often prefer to try products before buying, and some software providers take advantage of this preference. Qualcomm[27] widely distributes a freeware version of Eudora, an e-mail package. Customers who adopt the freeware version can easily upgrade to a commercial version, available for around $40, which offers some appealing additional features. In Qualcomm's case, the incentive to upgrade is increased functionality. Another approach is taken by game maker Storm Impact, which distributes TaskMaker[28] as freeware. The full functionality of the game is available to play the first two tasks; however, the next eight tasks require payment of $25. On receipt of payment, a registration code to unlock the remaining tasks is e-mailed so that the next task can be tackled immediately.

Word of mouth

Gossip and idle chatter around the water fountain are now complemented by lists and newsgroups. The impact of these electronic media can be quite profound as Intel discovered when the flaw in the Pentium chip was revealed in a message on the Internet. The incident was quickly conveyed to millions of Pentium customers, who bombarded Intel with e-mail. Indeed, Intel's CEO fueled discontent by posting an Internet message downplaying the problem and defending the company's decision to continue to produce defective chips. His Internet naivete (he used another executive's e-mail account to release the statement) was viewed negatively by the Internet community.

Word of mouth does not adequately describe the situation when a single electronic message can reach hundreds of thousands of people in a matter of minutes. It's more like a tsunami gathering momentum and crashing on the corporate doorstep before managers realize even a ripple of discontent. Bad news travels extremely fast on the Internet. Corporations are now monitoring lists and newsgroups that discuss their products and those of their competitors. As a result, they can quickly detect emerging problems and respond to statements that may be incorrect. Eavesdropping on customers' conversations is an important source of market intelligence, and it is becoming an important element of public relations.

27. http://www.qualcomm.com/
28. ftp://wuarchive.wustl.edu:system/mac/info-mac/game/task-maker-20.hqx

Public relations

When IBM[29] announced its takeover bid for Lotus,[30] it used the Internet to reach its stakeholders, media, and Lotus employees. Once the financial markets had been notified, IBM's Web page featured the letter from IBM CEO Louis Gerstner to Jim Manzi, Lotus CEO. Also included were the internal memo to IBM employees, press release, audio clip of Gerstner explaining the offer, and a transcript of Gerstner's 45-minute news conference. By the end of the day, 23,000 people had accessed the Web page—about double the normal traffic. In contrast, Lotus's page had a four-paragraph statement from Manzi, but a company spokesperson said Lotus would respond when it had more to say about the offer.[31]

As IBM demonstrated, the Web can be an effective public relations tool. The advantage is that a company can immediately transmit its message to stakeholders without relying on intermediaries, such as newspapers and TV, to redistribute messages. Of course, mass mailing is also a method for directly reaching stakeholders, but a letter lacks the recency and multimedia features of the Web. Now that IBM has led the way, expect to see greater use of the Web for public relations.

Products and services

The Web has become a popular medium for the distribution of product information. When Dell[32] announced a new range of notebook computers, its Web server received 16,000 hits in one day. Compaq[33] has installed a server to provide customers with technical support, free software patches, and upgrades. Offering product support through the Web provides several advantages. First, it's a 24-hour, global service. Regardless of geographic location, all customers with Web access can use the service. Second, its low cost; customers help themselves to the information they want. Third, customers can tailor their search to meet their needs, providing the supplier has a rich, structured Web site. Fourth, information can be easily updated as required. There are no out-of-date brochures.

Computer firms struggle to solve hardware and software problems for a multitude of customers. This is a problem that can easily spiral out of control. One approach is to let customers solve each other's problems. As sure as there is one customer with a problem, there is another who has solved it or who would love the opportunity to tackle a puzzler. If customers can be convinced to solve each other's problems, then this creates the possibility of lowering the cost of customer service and raising customer satisfaction levels.

Thus, the real task is to ensure that the customer with the problem finds the customer with the solution. Apple has developed a simple system for improving customer service by creating virtual groups who support each other, reducing the number of people that Apple has to support.

---

29. http://www.ibm.com/

30. http://www.lotus.com/

31. Adapted from: Associated Press. Internet industries: latest merger info on IBM-Lotus? Check cyberspace. *Athens Banner-Herald.* Athens, GA; June 8, 1995; A: 12.

32. http://www.dell.com/

33. http://www.compaq.com/

In December 1994, Apple established two electronic lists, one devoted to Macintosh Internet client software and the other dedicated to discussing Macintosh Internet server software. Apple set up the lists and announced their creation in a weekly electronic newsletter that reaches 140,000 Macintosh users. The lists have roughly 1,500 and 1,000 subscribers, respectively, and each averages 14 messages per day. Typically, a problem will receive several responses within a few hours. For example, the concise, smug answer to the problem posed in Figure 7-8 was posted two hours after the question appeared.

```
At 21:08 3/28/95, ... wrote:

>I would like to put our network on the internet before we get the ISDN or 56k

>line installed. Is it possible to use a 288 modem and put our small lan on the

>net. I know I can put one computer on use Config PPP but I want to put a few

>Macs on and keep the dial up connection up continuously.

>

ISP's modem ---[phone line]--- Modem ------ router ---[ethernet]--- LAN
Easy.
```

Figure 7-8. A list interaction

Quite encouraged by this venture, Apple now supports four lists, and the concept is being extended.

Popular culture    If you have seen *Forrest Gump,* you may remember the scene in which Forrest is riding his lawn mower. The maker's name is quite prominent for a few seconds. Firms have discovered that popular culture—movies, songs, and live performances—can be used to publicize their goods. As the Internet develops, we may see clearly labeled products appear in virtual network games. Indeed, a popular MUD (see page 123), Genocide, already features well-known fast food stores.[34]

## Efficiency

Renowned management scholar Peter Drucker observes that unless you measure the effect of a management action you cannot manage it. Thus, to manage a Web site, you need some measure of its efficiency. In practice, an organization may have different goals for its Web site, and multiple measures may be required.[35]

Organizations can have varying advertising and marketing objectives for establishing and maintaining a Web presence. One firm may wish to use the Web as a means of introducing itself and its products to potential customers.

---

34. As noted by Ned Watson, a teenage Internet addict.

35. This section is based on Berthon, P. R.; Pitt, L. F.; Watson, R. T. The World Wide Web as an advertising medium: towards an understanding of conversion efficiency. *Journal of Advertising Research.* 1996; 36(1): 43-54.

Its objective is to create corporate and product awareness and inform the market. On the other hand, if the customer knows of the firm and its products, then the company may want to use the Web site to process the customer's order. Another firm may be advertising and marketing well-known existing products, and its Web site objectives could be to solicit feedback from current customers as well as informing new customers. Thus, Web sites can be used to move customers and prospects through successive phases of the customer service life cycle. They do this by first attracting visitors, making contact with them (among those attracted), converting a portion of the interested contacts into interactive customers, and keeping them as customers.

Before we can define some measures of Web efficiency, we first need to define the variables to be measured (see Table 7-1). We also need to distinguish between hits and visitors. Merely hitting or landing on a site does not mean that the visitor did anything with the information to be found there—the visitor might simply hit and move on. An *active visit*, as compared to a hit, implies greater interaction between the visitor and the Web site. It may mean spending appreciable time (i.e., > x minutes) reading the page. Alternatively, it could be completing a form or querying a database. The overriding distinctive feature of a visit is some interaction between the visitor and the Web site.

Table 7-1: Web efficiency variables

| Variable | Meaning |
|---|---|
| $Q_0$ | Number of people with Web access |
| $Q_1$ | Number of people aware of the site |
| $Q_2$ | Number of hits on the site |
| $Q_3$ | Number of active visitors to the site |
| $Q_4$ | Number of purchases |
| $Q_5$ | Number of repurchases |

We now define six measures of Web site efficiency.

**Awareness:** Measures how effective an organization is in making those with Web access aware of its site. The awareness efficiency index is:

$$\text{awareness efficiency} = \eta_0 = \frac{\text{people aware of the site}}{\text{people with Web access}} = \frac{Q_1}{Q_0}$$

**Attractability:** Measures how effective an organization is in attracting aware people to its Web site. The attractability efficiency index is:

$$\text{attractability efficiency} = \eta_1 = \frac{\text{hits on the site}}{\text{people aware of the site}} = \frac{Q_2}{Q_1}$$

**Contact:** Measures how effectively the organization transforms Web site hits into visits.  The contact efficiency index is:

$$\text{contact efficiency} = \eta_2 = \frac{\text{active visitors to the site}}{\text{hits on the site}} = \frac{Q_3}{Q_2}$$

**Conversion:** Measures how effective an organization is in converting visitors into customers who place an order.  The conversion efficiency index is:

$$\text{conversion efficiency} = \eta_3 = \frac{\text{purchases}}{\text{active visitors}} = \frac{Q_4}{Q_3}$$

**Retention:** Measures how effective an organization is in getting customers to keep ordering.  The retention efficiency index is:

$$\text{retention efficiency} = \eta_4 = \frac{\text{repurchases}}{\text{purchases}} = \frac{Q_5}{Q_4}$$

**Web site:** Measures the overall efficiency of a Web site. The Web site efficiency index is:

$$\text{Web site efficiency} = \eta = \frac{1}{5}\sum_{1}^{5}\frac{Q_\eta}{Q_{\eta-1}}$$

The preceding measures provide Web site managers with some metrics for measuring performance. Depending on the objectives established for the site, some measures may be more relevant than others. For instance, an organization trying to establish its corporate image may be mainly interested in contact efficiency, while an on-line catalog may focus on retention.

## Your turn!

1. Estimate the awareness efficiency of Netscape's home page.
2. Estimate the attractability efficiency of Alta Vista, DEC's search engine.
3. What could your university or college do to increase the attractability of its Web site?
4. What might an organization do to increase the contact efficiency of its Web site?
5. What strategies might a firm use to increase conversion efficiency?
6. How might a firm increase retention efficiency?
7. Use a search engine to learn about Web page caching and consider its effect on each of the efficiency measures.

### Getting a grip on web advertising

Along with selling goods and products to those who visit their Web site, many organizations are looking for ways to place advertisements on popular Web sites. The Web has quickly become big business, with Web advertising expected to reach $110 million in 1996 and $1.86 billion by the year 2000. Of this ad revenue, about 75 percent is expected to go to 14 highly visited sites including CNN, ZD Net, and Yahoo! Given the amount of money that is now and will be spent on Web advertising, the companies placing the advertisements want to know what they are receiving for their money in terms of users actually viewing their ad. As a result, counting the number of Web visitors to an ad-supported Web site has become a business in and unto itself. Firms that track Web use must answer these questions: How many people saw the ad? Did they actually spend time reading it, or did they just surf right on by it?

The original standard of measure for Web use was the *hit*. Every time a Web file was requested by a user, that was considered a *hit*. However, with the high level of graphics on most Web pages today, it often takes many hits to download a single page. Other times, a visitor may terminate downloading the page without reading the advertisement. As a result, the number of hits does not directly correlate with the number of visitors to the Web page. Today, Web advertisers are demanding to know how many times the entire page was viewed, giving rise to a more precise unit of measurement known as the *page view*, *impression*, or *visit*. While most Web sites track their own visits, many advertisers don't rely on their numbers; this has generated a need for independent companies to measure Web visits in the same way that television and radio advertisers rely on Nielson and Arbitron ratings.

Another, even stricter unit of measure is the *click-through* rate; that is, how many times did the visitor to an ad-supported Web page actually click on an advertiser's hypertext link? This is like requiring that magazine advertising be measured based on the number of people who take the time to actually read an ad. However, Yahoo! recently signed a deal with Proctor and Gamble in which Yahoo! will be paid on a click-through-rate. Since this is a number that P&G can measure itself, it will not have to rely on an outside firm, thereby saving costs. As the Web grows and evolves, no doubt other measures will be tried as a way of measuring advertisement effectiveness.

Adapted from: Angwin, J. Firms vie to keep count of Web ads, *San Francisco Chronicle*, July 3, 1996:B1; and Heyman, K.Yahoo! puts its money on clicks, *Netguide*, July 1996:29.

## Conclusion

Electronic commerce offers many opportunities for organizations to redesign their present business practices. Many organizations, however, are not certain of where and how to start because they lack a systematic approach to redesign. The three models described in this chapter fill this gap. Managers now have some useful tools for strategic planning and identifying applications. By using the provided frameworks and examples of other companies' applications, businesses can set out to identify their opportunities. Of course, a good dose of Web surfing, just browsing around to get a feel for what's happening, might also lead to those serendipitous discoveries that provide elucidating glimpses into how an organization can exploit electronic commerce.

## Key terms and concepts

acquisition
adaptable Web site
adaptive Web site
attractability efficiency
attractor
awareness efficiency
contact efficiency
conversion efficiency
customer service life cycle

influence filter
Integrated Internet Marketing ($I^2M$)
ownership
requirements
retention efficiency
retirement
stakeholder
target refractor
Web site efficiency measure

## Exercises

1. Check out the *What's New?* link that you will find on many home pages and report any innovative uses of the Web. Do they fit the customer service life cycle or $I^2M$ model? If not, e-mail us so we can share your findings with other readers via this book's Web home page.

2. Meet with a business and, using the models in this chapter, help it brainstorm how it might use the Web.

3. Describe the approach you would use to increase the flow of innovative ideas from customers.

4. Identify some information-intensive products. How could the Web be used to promote them?

5. Identify some information-intensive services. How could the Web be used to promote these services?

6. What is RealAudio? How are firms using it to market their wares?

7. What is Pointcast? Should it be part of $I^2M$?

# A  Special Characters

| | | | | | | | |
|---|---|---|---|---|---|---|---|
| " | &quote; | Ê | &Ecirc; | Ò | &Ograve; |
| & | &amp; | ê | &ecirc; | ò | &ograve; |
| < | &lt; | È | &Egrave; | Ø | &Oslash; |
| > | &gt; | è | &egrave; | ø | &oslash; |
| Á | &Aacute; | Ë | &Euml; | Õ | &Otilde; |
| á | &aacute; | ë | &euml; | õ | &otilde; |
| Â | &Acirc; | fi | &THORN; | Ö | &Ouml; |
| â | &acirc; | fl | &thorn; | ö | &ouml; |
| À | &Agrave; | Í | &Iacute; | ß | &szlig; |
| à | &agrave; | í | &iacute; | Ú | &Uacute; |
| Å | &Aring; | Î | &Icirc; | ú | &uacute; |
| å | &aring; | î | &icirc; | Û | &Ucirc; |
| Ã | &Atilde; | Ì | &Igrave; | û | &ucirc; |
| ã | &atilde; | ì | &igrave; | Ù | &Ugrave; |
| Ä | &Auml; | Ï | &Iuml; | ù | &ugrave; |
| ä | &auml; | ï | &iuml; | Ü | &Uuml; |
| Æ | &AElig; | Ñ | &Ntilde; | ü | &uuml; |
| æ | &aelig; | ñ | &ntilde; | ÿ | &yuml; |
| Ç | &Ccedil; | Ó | &Oacute; | › | &eth; |
| ç | &ccedil; | ó | &oacute; | ‡ | &yacute; |
| É | &Eacute; | Ô | &Ocirc; | | |
| é | &eacute; | ô | &ocirc; | | |

# Glossary

**Absolute addressing.** A type of anchor address that indicates an object on a different server from the current Web page. The full URL must be specified in the anchor.

**Access control.** Techniques for controlling access to stored data or computer resources.

**Acquisition.** The second stage of the customer service life cycle during which the supplier helps the customer acquire a product or service.

**Adaptable Web site.** A site that can be customized by the visitor.

**Adaptive Web site.** A site that learns from the visitor's behavior and determines what should be presented.

**Advanced search.** A search mechanism that uses binary and unary operators to combine or negate search terms.

**Anchor.** A type of HTML tag that indicates the name of the object to be retrieved by the browser from a server.

**Anonymous FTP.** An FTP site that does not require users to have a user ID and password.

**Attractability efficiency.** Measures how effective an organization is in attracting aware people to its Web site.

**Attractor.** A web site that continually attracts a high number of visitors.

**Authentication.** The process of confirming the identity of a person or source of a message.

**Awareness efficiency.** Measures how effective an organization is in making those with Web access aware of its site.

**Background image.** A transparent images that servers as a form of *wallpaper* for the Web page.

**Backbone.** In a computer network, the primary high-speed communications link between major computer centers to which other networks are connected.

**Bandwidth.** The term used as a measure of the capacity of a communication channel, expressed in bits per second.

**Banner.** An advertisement that usually covers the bottom or top of a Web page.

**Bookmark.** A saved Web site URL.

**Browser.** Client software used on the Web to fetch and read documents on-screen and print them, jump to other documents via hypertext, view images, and listen to audio files.

**Browser button.** A button on the Navigator Gold toolbar that switches from the editor function to the browser function.

**Business service.** The software layer of electronic commerce that handles services required to support business transactions (e.g., encryption).

**Centralized computer network.** One in which there is one computer or a group of computers to which all other computers must be linked.

**Clickable map.** A graphical image on which sections act as hypertext links to other Web pages.

**Client.** A personal computer running an application that can access and display information on a server.

**Client/server computing.** A combination of clients and servers that provides the framework for distributing files across a network.

**Client-side map.** A clickable map that is processed by the browser rather than being sent to the server for processing.

**Codification.** An organized method for storing data in a computer system.

**Communication flip-flop.** A fundamental change in the nature of the relationship between buyers and servers caused by electronic commerce.

**Computer Network.** An interconnected system of computers.

**Contact efficiency.** Measures how effectively the organization transforms Web site hits into visits.

**Content area.** The part of the Netscape window in which the actual HTML-formatted text and inline images of the current page are displayed.

**Conversion efficiency.** Measures how effective an organization is in converting visitors into customers who place an order.

**Credit card.** A safe, secure and widely used remote payment system.

**Customer convergence.** The Web marketing concept that firms must describe their products and services so that potential customers converge on the relevant Web pages.

**Customer service life cycle.** A model that delineates the service relationship with a customer into four phases: requirements, acquisition, ownership, and retirement.

**Cyberspace.** Another name for the Internet and other forms of electronic communication.

**Data access control.** A method of controlling access to stored data.

**Decentralized computer network.** One in which there is no single computer or group of computers to which every other computer is linked.

**Decryption.** Conversion of encrypted text represented by characters into a readable form.

**Default Web page.** The Web page file that is accessed automatically at a Web site when no HTML file is shown as part of the URL.

**Demand risk.** The risk that changing demand or the collapse of markets significantly reduces demand for a firm's products or services.

**Digital cash or money.** An electronic form of money that is parallel to notes and coins.

**Directory buttons.** On the Netscape screen, a series of clickable buttons shown directly beneath the location window; they correspond to a special set of Web pages which the developers of Netscape believe to be useful to users.

**Discussion list.** A group of e-mail users who have all subscribed to a listserver to share their ideas on a particular topic.

**Disk cache.** In Netscape, the storage on disk of a number of recently visited Web pages.

**Distribution.** A measure of how widely information is shared.

**Divisibility.** The extent to which a currency can be divided into small units.

**Domain name.** Another name for the server computer address.

**Domain name service (DNS).** A system that keeps up with all Internet addresses.

**Download.** The process of moving software or data from a central computer to a personal computer and saving it on disk.

**Ecash.** An electronic payment system that can be used to withdraw and deposit ecash over the Internet. It provides the privacy of cash because the payer can remain anonymous.

**Electronic commerce.** Carrying out business transactions over computer networks.

**Electronic commerce application.** A computer interface between an organization and a stakeholder that is used to conduct transactions electronically.

**Electronic commerce topology.** The three types of communication networks used for electronic commerce: Internet, Intranet, and Interchain.

**Electronic communities.** Communities that are real in the sense that they are made of people, but electronic in the sense that all communication is in an electronic form.

**Electronic data interchange (EDI).** The electronic exchange of standard business documents between business partners.

**Electronic document.** An electronic form of a printed document.

**Electronic funds transfer (EFT).** The electronic movement of money.

**Electronic mail (e-mail).** An electronic technology that handles the sending and receiving of messages.

**Electronic publishing.** The electronic presentation of text and multimedia.

**Encryption.** The conversion of readable text into characters that disguise the original meaning of the text.

**File protocol.** The Web protocol used to access a local file.

**File transfer protocol (FTP).** A protocol that supports file transfers over the Internet.

**Firewall.** A device placed between an organization's network and the Internet to control data access.

**Forms.** Areas in Web pages that can be filled in by the user and returned to the Web server for processing.

**Frame.** A section of the browser window in which a Web page can be displayed.

**Frequently asked questions (FAQs).** A list of frequently asked questions about software or Web topics along with answers to the questions.

**Graphic elements.** The term encompassing several elements, including color, motion, and resolution, that together result in the ability of a computer to show line drawings, pictures, or animation on a display screen.

**Graphical user interface (GUI).** An interface that uses pictures and graphic symbols to represent commands, choices, or actions.

**Helper application.** Software packages linked to the browser in such a way that they are invoked automatically when the user requests that an audio or video file be played or a large image is displayed.

**History list.** A temporary list of recently visited Web pages.

**Home page.** The first page encountered at a Web site.

**Host computer.** A computer in a network that is connected to the Internet.

**Hypermedia.** An extension of hypertext that includes graphics, video, sound, and music.

**Hypertext.** A method of linking related information in which there is no hierarchy or menu system.

**Hypertext links.** Links to other Web pages or Internet resources.

**Hypertext markup language (HTML).** A markup language used to create Web pages consisting of text, hypertext links, and multimedia elements.

**Hypertext transfer protocol (http).** The protocol for moving hypertext files across the Internet.

**Inefficiency risk.** The risk that a firm loses market share because it fails to match competitors' unit costs.

**Influence filter.** A method of making a Web site more attractive to stakeholders.

**Information intensity.** The degree of information required to describe completely a product or service.

**Innovation risk.** The risk that a firm fails to continually improve its products and services and loses market share to more innovative competitors.

**Integrated Internet marketing ($I^2M$).** The coordination of Internet facilities to market products and services, shape stakeholder attitudes, and establish or maintain a corporate image.

**Interchain.** An electronic connection using Internet technology linking business partners to facilitate greater coordination of common activities. The term is derived from *Inter*net and the value *chain*.

**Internet.** A worldwide network of computers and computer networks in private organizations, government institutions, and universities, over which people share files, send electronic messages, and have access to vast quantities of information.

**Internet newsgroups.** See **newsgroups**.

**Internet operations.** A variety of operations that can be carried out on the Internet including FTP, e-mail, telnet, newsgroups, and the World Wide Web.

**Internet service providers.** Companies that specialize in linking organizations and individuals to the Internet as well as providing services to them.

**Intranet.** An intra-organizational network based on using Internet technology. It enables people within the organization to communicate and cooperate with each other.

**List.** A type of HTML tag that creates three types of lists: regular, menu, and descriptive.

**Listserver.** A program providing a set of e-mail functions that enables users to participate in electronic discussions.

**Local area network (LAN).** A computer network that is restricted to one geographical area.

**Local files.** Web files that are available from a local hard disk or network file server.

**Location window.** A text window located immediately beneath the toolbar in which the URL of the current page is displayed. It also can be used to enter a new URL.

**Logical style.** HTML syntax for specifying how a text string will be displayed by a browser. Each command corresponds to a logical representation of text (e.g., emphasis) that may be changed by the user of the browser (e.g., display *emphasis* as *bold*).

**Mail indicator.** An envelope icon at the bottom right hand corner of the screen that indicates whether or not you have mail waiting to be read.

**Many-to-many communication.** A form of communication in which many people can communicate with many other persons.

**Map.** See **clickable map**.

**Market segmentation.** The division of a market into segments based on demographic or other relevant variables in order to deliver more precisely an appropriate message to potential customers.

**Markup language.** A publishing industry term for describing the size, style, and position of each typographical element on a page.

**Mass marketing.** Broadcasting the same message to all potential customers.

**Memory cache.** In Netscape, the storage of recent Web pages in computer memory.

**Menu bar.** A menu bar at the top of the Netscape screen that provides users with a variety of options from which to choose.

**Message distribution.** The software layer of electronic commerce that sends and receives messages.

**Modem.** A communications device that modulates computer signals into outgoing audio signals and demodulates incoming audio signals into computer signals.

**Mouse pointer.** The icon on the screen that represents the current location on the screen; usually an arrow or pointing finger.

**Multimedia.** A interactive combination of text, graphics, animation, images, audio, and video displayed by and under the control of a personal computer.

**Multimedia files.** Digitized images, videos, and sound that can be retrieved and converted into an appropriate human recognizable information by a client.

**Multipurpose Internet mail extension (MIME).** A protocol that is a widely used for the interchange of files.

**Multi-user dimension or dungeon (MUD).** A multiple-user electronic game that is an ongoing drama with an electronically assembled cast exploring and interacting in cyberspace.

**National information infrastructure.** A nation's communication networks, including the TV and radio broadcast industries, cable TV, telephone networks, cellular communication systems, computer networks, and the Internet.

**Newsgroups.** A vast set of discussion lists that can be accessed through the Internet.

**One-to-one marketing.** Delivering a specific message to a particular customer, often assisted by a marketing database.

**Opening home page.** The Web page that is automatically loaded when Netscape is first accessed or the Home Toolbar button is clicked.

**Ownership.** The third stage of the customer service life cycle during which the supplier helps the customer maintain a product or service.

**Page.** An electronic document on the Web that contains text and hypertext links to multimedia elements and other pages that are stored on server computers.

**Path.** A portion of the URL which includes the name of the home page file plus any directories or folders in which it is located.

**Physical style.** A HTML syntax for specifying how a text string will be displayed by a browser. Each command corresponds to a physical representation of text (e.g., bold) that cannot be changed by the user of the browser.

**Plug-in.** An extension that provides seamless support for data types not supported by the browser.

**Point and click navigation.** A method that involves using a mouse or other pointing device to position the pointer over a hypertext link or the menu bar, tool bar, location window, or directory buttons and clicking a button to retrieve a Web page or execute a corresponding command.

**Point and click operations.** Operations that can be carried out simply by pointing at menu selections or icons representing operations and clicking the mouse button.

**Pop-up menu.** A mini-menu that appears on the Netscape screen when the right mouse button is clicked.

**Port number.** An internal address within a Web server.

**Portable document format (PDF).** A form of electronic document created with Adobe's Acrobat Exchange that can be easily shared with anyone who has an Acrobat reader.

**Private key.** A encryption key that is known only by the person sending and receiving encrypted messages.

**Progress bar.** An area at the bottom of the Netscape screen which uses both text and graphics to display the status of loading a Web page as well as to display other useful information.

**Protocol.** A formal set of rules for specifying the format and relationships when exchanging information between communicating devices.

**Proximity search.** A search that looks for words that are "close" to one another.

**Public key.** A encryption key that is known to all persons who share encrypted communication with a particular person (who holds a private key).

**Publish button.** A button on the Navigator Gold toolbar that saves the Web page to a local disk.

**Relative addressing.** A type of anchor address that indicates an object on the same server as the Web page. Only the path portion of the URL is specified in the anchor.

**Requirements.** The first stage of the customer service life cycle during which the supplier helps the customer determine the attributes of the required product or service.

**Retention efficiency.** Measures how effective an organization is in getting customers to keep ordering.

**Retirement.** The fourth and final stage of the customer service life cycle during which the supplier helps the customer dispose of a product or service.

**Routing.** The process of determining the path a message will take from the sending to the receiving computer.

**Scroll bars.** Horizontal and vertical bars in a browser that allow movement to parts of the Web page that are not currently on the screen.

**Search engines.** Software that has been developed to enable Web users to search for Web pages that contain desired topics.

**Secure server.** A Web server that provides users protection from having their messages read while being transmitted over the Internet.

**Security.** The process of protecting stored data and transported messages.

**Security area.** An area of the Netscape screen that displays a door key; if the door key is displayed on a blue background, then the home page is considered secure.

**Server.** A computer on the Web running an application that manages a data store containing files of text, images, video clips, and sound.

**Server address.** The address of the computer on which the Web resource is stored.

**Server side map.** A clickable map that is sent to the server computer for processing rather than being processed by the browser.

**Service resource.** Another name for a protocol on the Web.

**Shortcut keys.** Key combinations that can be used instead of the mouse button; often uses the Ctrl key in conjunction with a letter.

**Signed message.** A message that can be authenticated as being from a particular person.

**Simple search.** A search that looks for words or terms without any binary or unary operators.

**Smart card.** A card, containing memory and a microprocessor, that can serve as personal identification, credit card, ATM card, telephone credit card, critical medical information record, and as cash for small transactions.

**Sniffer.** A network program that hackers use to intercept and reads messages on the Internet.

**Special characters.** Non-ASCII characters that are created by HTML in the form &charactername; where & indicates the beginning of the character and ; indicates the end.

**Stakeholder.** Some person or group that can determine the future of an organization.

**Status indicator.** An area of the Netscape screen in which the Netscape corporate logo is displayed; it is animated in some way while a Web page is being loaded.

**Style tag.** HTML tags that define how text will appear when displayed by a browser.

**Table.** A type of HTML tag that supports the presentation of a table containing a caption, column, row headers, and cell elements.

**Tag.** The basic component of HTML which describes to the Web browser how to display information.

**Target refractor.** A method for customizing a Web site to meet the needs of stakeholders.

**Transmission control protocol/Internet protocol (TCP/IP).** The communication protocol of the Internet.

**Telnet.** The main Internet protocol for connecting to a remote machine.

**Text (ASCII) file.** A file in the form of readable text, as opposed to binary.

**Title bar.** The area at the top of the Netscape screen that displays the title of the current Web page.

**Toolbar.** A button bar located beneath the menu bar which consists of nine command buttons that provide quick access to important Netscape operations.

**Uniform resource locator (URL).** A standard means of consistently locating Web pages or other resources no matter where they are stored on the Internet.

**Value-added network (VAN).** A network that offers services over and above those furnished by common carriers. Often used to support EDI.

**Value chain.** The chain of business activities in which each activity adds value to the end product or service.

**Web directory.** A hierarchically structured list of Web pages. Available from Netscape by clicking on the Net Directory button.

**Web page.** A special type of document that contains hypertext links to other documents or to various multimedia elements.

**Web page address.** The Internet address at which a Web page is found.

**Web searching.** The process of searching for Web pages of interest using a piece of software called a search engine.

**Web site.** An Internet server on which Web pages are stored.

**Web site efficiency.** A measure for assessing the efficiency of a Web site.

**World Wide Web (WWW).** A body of software, a set of protocols, and conventions based on hypertext and multimedia techniques that make the Internet easy for anyone to browse and add contributions.

# Index

electronic fund transfer
(EFT) 147
electronic money 146–149
electronic publishing 120
e-mail 40, 109–111
address 88
Netscape Navigator 49, 60
reading 111
sending 110
encryption 142, 143
ESPNet 108
Eudora 164
Extranet 141

**F**
FAQs (frequently asked
questions) 108
Federal Express 153
file protocol 34
Firefly 153
firewall 135, 141
forms 38, 92
Forrest Gump 166
FrameMaker 80
frames 66–70, 95
France 148
FTP (file transfer protocol) 80,
116

**G**
General Electric 133
General Motors 129
geographic database server 118
Global Recycling Network
(GRN) 159
Goodyear Tire & Rubber 153
graphic elements 28
GUI (graphical user interface) 30

**H**
Häagen-Dazs 4
helper 35, 118
Hewlett Packard 155
home page 26
HTML
address tag 79
anchor 84
block quote 79
body tag 75
comments 77
descriptive list 82
electronic document 121–123
frames 95
FTP 117
head tag 75
heading level 76
horizontal rule 77

html tag 75
hypertext markup
language 26,73
line break 76
linking to another
document 86, 87
linking within a document 85
lists 81
loading an image 88
logical styles 79
mailto 88
map 93
menu list 82
ordered list 81
paragraph 76
physical styles 78
preformatted tag 79
regular list 81
style tag 78
telnet 117
transportability 87
typewriter tag 78
HTML file
default 32
HTTP (hypertext transfer
protocol) 31
hyperlink 74
hypertext 22, 74
defined 10

**I**
IBM 165
image 84, 88
alignment options 89
industrial marketing 133
inefficiency risk 131
information intensity 133
InfoSeek Guide 37
infrastructure 127–128
initial public offering (IPO) 121
innovation risk 130
Integrated Internet
marketing 160–166
Intel 160, 164
Interchain 136, 137–140
Internal Revenue Service 122
Internet 6–9, 135
access 8
backbone 8
history 7
operations 7
problems 23
Internet Network Information
Center (InterNIC) 126
Internet service provider (ISP) 8
inter-organizational system
(IOS) 140

Intranet 135
IP address 126
ISWorld Net 161

**J**
Jimmy Buffett 18
JobDirect 102
JobWeb 102

**K**
Kellogg's Company 152
Kodak 108

**L**
Lane and Lenge 156
lead testing kit 156
line break 76
linking within a document 85
listserv 113
local file 33, 51
Lotus 165

**M**
Macromedia 120
Magellan 104
Manheim Auctions 139, 163
many-to-many
communication 3
map 40, 93
client-side processing 94
definition file 93
server-side processing 93
Margaritaville 18
Mark Twain Bank of
Missouri 148
markup language 26, 73
Mayo Clinic 153
Microsoft 135, 149
Internet Explorer 26
Word 80
MIME (multipurpose Internet
mail extension) 119
Mosaic 23
MUD (multiple user
dungeon) 123, 166
multimedia 11, 74

**N**
Net Directory 107
Net Search 103
Netscape
browser button 99
publish button 99
Netscape Navigator 26, 41–44,
47–51, 103
content area 27
directory buttons 66